Dates and Meanings of Religious and Other Festivals

With a calendar for 1997-2001

John G. Walshe M.A., Dip RE. Ph.D.
and
Shrikala Warrier M.A., Ph.D.

foulsham educational

LONDON • NEW YORK • TORONTO • SYDNEY

foulsham

The Publishing House,
Bennetts Close, Cippenham,
Slough, Berks SL1 5AP

ISBN 0-572-02322-7

Typeset in Great Britain by Typesetting Solutions, Slough, Berks.
Printed in Great Britain by Redwood Books, Trowbridge, Wiltshire.

Dates and Meanings of Religious and Other Festivals

With a calendar for 1997-2001

Contents

Acknowledgements

During the course of nearly two decades, in which this publication has evolved from an idea for a resource for teachers to a book intended for a much wider audience, many people have contributed to its accomplishment. We owe an immense debt of gratitude to former students and colleagues in Ealing's Community Education Team for useful factual information and advice in putting together the earlier versions.

For this publication, however, we particularly wish to acknowledge the contributions of the following:

Mr Bahadar Singh, The Sikh Missionary Society

Pandit Narottam Pandey, Sree Ram Mandir, Southall

The Central Mosque, Regent's Park, London

The Buddhist Society, London

The Tibet Foundation, London

The Board of Deputies of British Jews

National Spiritual Assembly of the Baha'is of the United Kingdom

Mr John Gauss, Ealing Central Library

Dr Ela Shah

Mrs Ammu Warrier, Chinmaya Mission Society, Bangalore, India

David Tennant, Education Consultant

Rev Thomas Hardy, Retired Clergyman

Rev Perry Gildea C.M., St Mary's College, Twickenham

Mr G.U. Syed, Central Jamia Mosque, Southall

It has been a pleasure to work again with W. Foulsham & Co. Ltd.

London, 1997

John G. Walshe and
Shrikala Warrier

Foreword

I am delighted to be able to write this Foreword to a most invaluable piece of work which provides an underpinning to the good understanding of the major faiths in the United Kingdom.

In 1988, the Education Reform Act made it a statutory requirement for all schools to study Christianity and all other principal faiths and this led to the School Curriculum and Assessment Authority bringing together key leaders of different faiths and communities to provide working group reports. These reports provide the basis of an authentic and sensitive approach to teaching world religions in the context of an increasingly multicultural society.

Dates and Meanings of Religious and Other Festivals provides an excellent background information, but above all it provides this information in a format that respects the integrity of each faith.

It is this contribution to quality in Religious Education that will provide many institutions with the confidence and competence to learn about, and from, religion.

I hope that those who have received this book will welcome it as a vital means of understanding the religious and cultural needs of individuals within their organisations.

LAURIE ROSENBERG
Executive Director
Office of the Chief Rabbi
London

Publisher's Note

Every effort has been made through a worldwide spread of advisers to confirm all the religious and feast days over the next five years.

Many of the celebrations are movable feasts – some based on lunar reckonings. Thus, some of the dates are approximations and others, particularly after the turn of the century, are not yet known by the relevant authorities.

The publishers will be keeping a database of up-to-date information and would welcome enquiries from schools and others wishing to check any dates with us.

Please telephone 01753 526769

Calendars

The calendar is a method of adjusting the natural divisions of time with respect to one another for both administrative purposes and for the observance of religious festivals. The term 'calendar' is derived from the Latin word 'kalendae' which designated the first day of the month in Roman times.

Celestial bodies provide the basic standard for determining the calendar. The basic calendar units are the day, month and year, derived from the movements of the earth, the moon and the sun respectively.

A Day

A day is measured by the rotation of the earth on its axis. The duration of one complete rotation with respect to the stars is called the sidereal day (from the Latin 'sidus' which means 'star') a unit of time that is important in astronomy.

The cycle of night and day has considerable bearing on man's life. Hence, the solar day, or the interval between two passages of the sun across the meridian, is the basis of the civil calendar. The solar day is longer than the sidereal day by approximately four minutes.

A Month

A lunar month is the time it takes the moon to complete a cycle of phases. It has an average length of 29.5 days.

A Year

A year corresponds to the cycle of the seasons and is the result of the sun's apparent movement through the constellations of the zodiac as the earth moves around the sun.

The astronomical year is defined as the movement of the sun over the earth's hemisphere. The instant when the centre of the sun's disk crosses the equator is known as the vernal equinox, and the time interval between two vernal equinoxes is known as the seasonal or tropical year. A year averages 365 days.

A Week

The week is a calendar unit that is almost universally used. It is an artificial unit of time, although its length of seven days relates it to the phases of the moon. The Hebrews were the first to use it. In most languages the days of the week are named after the seven moving celestial objects that were known in ancient times, namely the Sun, Moon, Mars, Mercury, Jupiter, Venus and Saturn.

Types of Calendars

There are three basic types of calendars: the lunar, lunisolar and solar, based on the phases of the moon and the apparent movements of the sun.

Lunar Calendar

The oldest kind of calendar is the lunar calendar. In this type, the civil month is approximately the same length as the actual lunar month, and the first day of each civil month coincides with the new moon.

To establish agreement between the civil month, composed of a whole number of days, and the lunar month of 29.5306 days, an early solution was to have civil months that were alternately 29 and 30 days long. This made for an average civil month of 29.5 days – a lag of 0.0306 days behind the actual lunar month. Later lunar calendars grouped twelve civil months in a lunar year of 365 days. The year therefore lagged behind the cycle of the moon's phases by 0.3672 days. One way of compensating fairly precisely for this lag was to insert one day in the calendar (intercalate) every three years. Alternative solutions were to intercalate three days over a period of eight years, seven days in nineteen years, or eleven days in thirty years.

Lunisolar Calendars

Once the significance of the solar year of 365.25 days came to be recognised, an exact relationship was sought between the solar year and the lunar month. One of the first solutions was to add a month to every three years. Alternatively, if three months are added to eight lunar years or seven months to nineteen lunar years, the adjustment closely approximates to eight or nineteen solar years respectively. Both the eight-year (Octennial) cycle and the nineteen-year (Metonic) cycle were used by the ancient Greeks. The Metonic cycle is fairly precise and is still used in ecclesiastical calendar calculations.

Solar Calendars

In modern times, the lunar month has been largely rejected in order to ensure better agreement between the civil month and the solar year. The twelve months are retained but are no longer lunar, so that the new moon may fall on any day of the month. Only the value of 365.2422 days as the average length of the year is fundamental to the establishment of the solar calendar.

A year of 365 days came to be used with an additional day intercalated every fourth year. The intercalary year was designated the leap year. This was the solution adopted in the Julian calendar. However, as the fraction to be compensated for is, in fact, 0.2422 days and not 0.25 days, an addition of one day every four years results in an excess of 0.0078 days per year and a cumulative error of about three days every four centuries. The Gregorian reforms which resulted in the modern Western calendar eliminates, to a large extent, this remaining discrepancy.

The Western Calendar

The Western calendar had its origin in the desire for a solar calendar that kept in step with the seasons and possessed fixed rules of intercalation. With the rise of Christianity, it also had to provide a method of dating movable religious feasts such as Easter which were based on lunar reckoning. To reconcile the lunar and solar schemes, features of the Roman Republican calendar and the Egyptian calendar were used.

The early Romans used a lunar calendar in which the lengths of the months alternated between 29 and 30 days. The civil year was composed of ten months and therefore of 295 days. The first month in the calendar was March. The seventh, eighth, ninth and tenth months were named September, October, November and December – Latin words indicating the position of these months in the year.

According to legend, it was around 700 BC that January and February were added as the eleventh and twelfth months of the year. February consisted of only 28 days.

In the course of time, the Roman Republican calendar became increasingly out of step with the seasons. A need therefore arose for a calendar that would allow the months to be based on phases of the moon and the year to be in line with the seasons.

The reformation of the Roman calendar was undertaken by Julius Caesar in 46 BC. The lunar calendar was abandoned. Instead, the months were arranged on a seasonal basis and the solar year was used, with its length taken as 365¼ days.

It was also decided that the vernal equinox would fall on March 25. The civil year was fixed at 365 days and an additional day was intercalated every four years so that the solar year would remain in agreement with the seasons. The extra day was added after February 28.

The Julian reforms also reinstated January 1 as the first day of the year. January 45 BC thus inaugurates the Julian calendar. A discrepancy in names was retained, however, in that the months of September to December still had their former names, although they were now the ninth to the twelfth months of the year.

The Gregorian Calendar

The average length of the year in the Julian calendar, fixed at 365¼ days, is eleven minutes longer than the solar year. There was thus a cumulative error amounting to nearly eight days in the course of 1000 years, and the calendar once again became increasingly out of phase with the seasons.

In 1582, Pope Gregory XIII reformed the Julian calendar by shortening the year by ten days to bring the vernal equinox to March 21. It was further ordained that no centennial years should be leap years unless they were exactly divisible by 400. Thus, 1700, 1800 and 1900 were not leap years although the year 2000 is. The reform measures also laid down the rules for calculating the date of Easter.

Easter was the most important feast of the Christian Church and its place in the calendar determined the position of the rest of the Church's movable feasts. Its timing depended on both the moon's phases and the vernal equinox. Church authorities therefore had to seek some way of reconciling the lunar and solar calendars.

Easter was primarily designated a spring festival, and the earliest Christians celebrated it at the same time as the Jewish Passover festival, that is during the night of the first full moon of the first month of spring (Nisan 14 and 15). By the middle of the second century, most Churches had transferred this celebration to the Sunday after the Passover feast. The Council of Nicea observed the feast on a Sunday. Yet many disparities remained in fixing the date of Easter. Today the Eastern Churches follow the Julian calendar and the Western Churches the Gregorian calendar, so that in some years there may be a month's difference in the times of celebration.

The Gregorian calendar was adopted exactly according to the mandate of the Pope in France, Spain, Portugal and Italy in 1582. The Protestant countries, however, were slow to adopt it. In England it was not adopted until 1752.

The Eastern Orthodox Church

In 1054 a split occurred between the four Eastern patriarchates and the Roman (Western) patriarchate. The Orthodox Eastern Church, also known as the Orthodox Church and the Greek Orthodox Church, is the federation of thirteen autocephalous (i.e. 'having their own heads') Orthodox Churches chiefly in Greece, Cyprus, Romania, Bulgaria, some of the independent states of the former Soviet Union and the Middle East. Together they comprise about one-sixth of the world's Christian population.

Slavic Orthodoxy

In the middle of the ninth century two Greek brothers, Constantine and Methodios, were sent to bring Christianity to Slavic lands. Before they began, the scholarly brother, Constantine, translated most of the New Testament and the Orthodox Service books into Slavonic. To do this Constantine developed a new alphabet. When he became a monk, he changed his name to Cyril – so the alphabets to this day used by, for example, Russians, Serbs, Bulgarians and Ukrainians are called Cyrillic.

Russian Orthodoxy

Towards the end of the tenth century, Vladimir, Prince of Kiev, invited Orthodox missionaries from Constantinople to teach his people. His grandmother, Olga, was a Christian, and he was to marry a Christian princess from Byzantium. The mission met with spectacular success: Greek clergy performed a mass baptism in the river at Kiev in AD 988, and Orthodox Christianity spread rapidly among the people called 'Rus'.

The Russian Primary Chronicle gives an account of how Vladimir, in his pagan days, chose Orthodoxy. He sent envoys to view the various nations at worship. Those who went to the Cathedral of the Holy Wisdom in Constantinople were transfixed by the glory of the service: "We knew not whether we were in heaven or on earth; but this we know, that God dwells there among them".

The Orthodox Church Calendar

The Calendar reform by Pope Gregory XIII in 1582 was rejected by the Orthodox Church who viewed the papal reform as divisive and lacking in due respect for the traditions and oneness of the Church. The enforcement of the Gregorian calendar by several temporal rulers was regarded without enthusiasm.

Since 1923, the Orthodox Church has been divided over the calendar. In that year several churches (mainly Greek) decided to adopt the new calendar for all days except the days that depend on Easter. Easter is still to be reckoned by the old calendar.

Those (mostly Slavic) churches who retain the Julian calendar remain thirteen days behind other Christians in the determining of festival dates. As examples: old-style Christmas falls on January 7 and New Year's day falls on January 14 in the Gregorian calendar.

The Hindu Calendar

While the Republic of India has adopted the Gregorian calendar for secular purposes, the religious life of Hindus continues to be governed by the traditional Hindu calendar, which is based primarily on the lunar cycle but adapted to solar reckoning.

The oldest form of the Hindu calendar is known from texts of about 1000 BC. It divides a solar year of approximately 360 days into twelve lunar months. In order to align it with the solar year of 365 days, a leap month was intercalated every 60 months.

The year was divided into three periods of four months, each of which would be introduced by a special religious rite, the 'Chaturmasya' (four-month rite). Each of these periods was further divided into two parts (seasons or 'rtu'):

Spring	Vasantha	Mid-February to mid-April
Summer	Grishma	Mid-April to mid-June
Rainy Season	Varsa	Mid-June to mid-August
Autumn	Sarad	Mid-August to mid-October
Winter	Hemanta	Mid-October to mid-December
Dewy Season	Sisira	Mid-December to mid-February

The month, counted from full moon to full moon, was divided into two parts (paksha) of waning (krsna paksha) and waxing (sukla-paksha) and special rituals were prescribed on the days of the new moon (amavasya) and full moon (purnima). The lunar day (tithi), a thirtieth part of the lunar month, was reckoned to be the basic unit of the calendar. However, as the lunar month is only about 29½ solar days, the tithi does not correspond with the natural day of 24 hours.

The 'Jyotisa-Vedanga', a treatise on time reckoning dated around 100 BC, adds a larger unit of five years (yuga) to these divisions. A further distinction was made between the uttarayana (northern course), when the sun rises every morning farther north, and dakshinayana (southern course), when it rises progressively south.

The reckoning in general, was mostly dictated by the requirements of rituals, the time of which had to be fixed correctly. When astrology came into vogue for casting horoscopes and making predictions, zodiacal time measurement was introduced into the calendar.

The year began with the entry of the sun (sankranti) in the sign of Aries. The names of the zodiacal signs (rasi) were taken over and translated into Sanskrit. The table below indicates the zodiacal signs in the Hindu calendar and their Western equivalents.

Mesa	Ram	Aries
Vrsabha	Bull	Taurus
Mithuna	Twins	Gemini
Karkata	Crab	Cancer
Simha	Lion	Leo
Kanya	Maiden	Virgo
Tula	Scale	Libra
Vrschika	Scorpion	Scorpio
Dhanus	Bow	Sagittarius
Makara	Crocodile	Capricorn
Kumbha	Water jar	Aquarius
Mina	Fish	Pisces

While the solar system has significance for astrology, time for ritual purposes continues to be reckoned by the lunar calendar. The names of the months in this system are as follows:

Chaitra	March–April	
Vaisakha	April–May	
Jyaistha	May–June	
Ashada	June–July	
Sravana	July–August	
Bhadrapada	August–September	
Asvina	September–October	
Karthika	October–November	
Margasirsa	November–December	
Pausa	December–January	
Magha	January–February	
Phalguna	February–March	

In the course of time, India also adopted the seven-day week (saptaha) from the West and the days were named after the corresponding planets.

Sunday	Ravivara	Sun
Monday	Somavara	Moon
Tuesday	Mangalvara	Mars
Wednesday	Budhvara	Mercury
Thursday	Brihspativara	Jupiter
Friday	Sukravara	Venus
Saturday	Sanivara	Saturn

The Eras

There is no evidence that before the first century BC, the years of events were recorded in well-defined eras.

Among those which have remained influential are the Vikrama Era (begun in 58 BC), the Saka Era (which commenced from AD 78), the Gupta Era (commenced from AD 320) and the Harsha Era (which began from AD 606). All these were dated from some significant historical event, though the first two are the most commonly used.

In the Hindu calendar, the date of an event takes the following form: month, fortnight (either waxing or waning moon), name (usually the number) of the tithi in that fortnight and the year of the particular era which the writer follows.

Important Hindu festivals are usually based on the lunar calendar. However, the sun's entry into the sign of Aries, marking the beginning of the astrological year, and the sun's entry into the sign of Capricorn (makara sankranti), marking the winter solstice, are also regarded as important days in the calendar. The latter coincides with a harvest festival, which in the southern Indian state of Tamil Nadu is widely celebrated as the Pongal Festival.

The Muslim Calendar

The Muslim Era commences from the year of Hegira (AD 622) – the migration of the Prophet Mohammed and his followers from Mecca to Medina. The second caliph, Omar I, who reigned AD 634–644, set the first day of the month Muharram as the beginning of the year.

The Muslim calendar is based on the lunar cycle and consists of twelve months alternating 30 and 29 days each. The first day of each month is determined by the sighting of the new moon. The year is reckoned to have 354 days, but the last month, Dhu-al-hijjah (Zul-Hijja) sometimes has an intercalated day, bringing it up to 30 days and a total of 355 days for that year. The Muslim calendar is therefore eleven days shorter than the Gregorian calendar year.

Although the Christian Era may be in official use, people in Muslim countries tend to use the Muslim Era for non-official purposes. To calculate conversions from the Muslim to the Gregorian calendar, the following formula is used:

$$G = H + 622 - \frac{H}{33}$$

$$H = G - 622 + \frac{G - 622}{32}$$

G = Gregorian calendar
H = Hegira

The names of the months in the Muslim calendar and the number of days in each are listed below.

	Name	Length
1	Muharram	30 days
2	Safar	29 days
3	Rabee ul-Awwal	30 days
4	Rabee ul-Thani	29 days
5	Jumadi ul-Awwal	30 days
6	Jumadi ul-Thani	29 days
7	Rajab	30 days
8	Shaban	29 days
9	Ramadhan	30 days
10	Shawwal	29 days
11	Zul-Qeda	30 days
12	Zul-Hijja	29 days

The first month (Muharram), the seventh (Rajab) and the last two (Zul-Qeda and Zul-Hijja) are considered sacred months. Ramadhan, the ninth month of the Muslim calendar, is observed throughout the Muslim world as a period of fasting. According to the Holy Quran, Muslims must see the new moon with the naked eye before they can begin their fast. Should the new moon prove difficult to sight then the month Shaban, immediately preceding Ramadhan, will be reckoned to have 30 days and the fast will commence on the day following the last day of Shaban.

'The number of months with Allah has been twelve by Allah's ordinance since the day he created the heavens and the earth. Of these, four are known as sacred.'
(The Holy Quran 9:36)

'They ask thee, O Prophet, concerning the phases of the moon. Tell them: these alterations are a means of determining time for regulation of people's affairs and for the pilgrimage.'
(The Holy Quran 2:190)

The solar system of reckoning time is used as the basis for the five daily prayers as well as for determining the beginning and breaking of the fast during Ramadhan. When worship is to be completed within a particular month or part of a month, the lunar system is used, as in the determination of the month of fasting or fixing the time of Haj – the pilgrimage. Islamic festivals, however, are based on lunar sightings rather than lunar reckonings. It is therefore not possible to have the exact dates of these festivals very much in advance.

The Jewish Calendar

The Jewish calendar in use today is lunisolar, the years being solar and the month lunar. The year consists of twelve months which are alternately 29 and 30 days in length. In order to celebrate the festivals in their proper season, the difference between the lunar year (354 days) and the solar year (365½ days) is made up by intercalating a thirteenth month of 30 days in the third, sixth, eighth, eleventh, fourteenth, seventeenth and nineteenth year of a nineteen-year cycle. The month so added is called Adar Sheni (second Adar) and the year, a leap year. The intercalary year can contain 383, 384 or 385 days, while ordinary years contain 353, 354 or 355 days.

The year commences at the new moon of Tishri (September to October) but its beginning may be shifted by a day for various reasons, among them the rule that the Day of Atonement must not fall on a Friday or Sunday, the seventh day of Tabernacles or a sabbath.

The months are counted (following a biblical custom) from Nisan. Only a few biblical month names are known. The present ones are of Babylonian origin.

The Jewish Era in use today is dated from the supposed year of the creation, calculated on biblical data to coincide with 3761 BC. In giving Hebrew dates, it is customary to use Hebrew letters for numbers and to omit the thousands from the year number.

The Hebrews can be considered to have established the week as a unit of time. The pivot of the week is the sabbath, or day of rest, which corresponds to Saturday in the modern calendar.

For practical purposes, for example, for reckoning the commencement of the sabbath, the day begins at sunset. The calendar day of 24 hours, however, always begins at 6 p.m.

The names of the months in the Hebrew calendar and the number of days in each are listed below.

	Hebrew Name	Babylonian Name	Length
1	Nisan	Nisannu	30 days
2	Iyyar	Ayaru	29 days
3	Sivan	Shimanu	30 days
4	Tammuz	Du'uzu	29 days
5	Av	Abu	30 days
6	Ellul	Ululu	29 days
7	Tishri	Tashretu	30 days
8	Marheshvan (Heshvan)	Arakshanana	29/30 days
9	Kislev	Kishnuu	29/30 days
10	Tevet	Tabetu	29/30 days
11	Shevat	Shabatu	30 days
12	Adar	Addaru	29 days
			(30 days in leap year)

The Buddhist Calendar

The Buddhist calendar combines solar and lunar elements. The year is solar, usually consisting of twelve months, with the inclusion of an additional month every four or five years. All religious festivals, however, follow the lunar calendar.

The full moon days in each month are important to Buddhists and many of them are celebrated with colourful ceremonies. The full moon day in the month of Vesakha (Vaisakha) is particularly significant in Theravada Buddhist countries such as Sri Lanka and Thailand, as it commemorates the birth, enlightenment and death of the Buddha. Followers of the Mahayana and Zen traditions normally celebrate each of these events on separate days.

The Buddhist calendar tends to vary from one country to another, and from one school of Buddhism to another. In Sri Lanka, Nepal and south-east Asian countries such as Thailand, the year begins on a fixed date in April. The Chinese and Tibetan New Year's Day, however, falls at a new moon. Chinese New Year is usually celebrated in the second half of January or the first half of February. The Tibetan New Year, Losar, usually falls in February. The exact date varies from year to year.

In Britain the three main schools in order of arrival are Theravada, Zen and Tibetan. In Pali, the ancient North Indian language, the names of the Buddhist months are:

Citta	Assayuja
Vesaka	Kattika
Jettha	Maggasira
Asalha	Pussa
Savana	Maga
Potthabada	Phagguna

The additional or thirteenth month is called Adhivesaka.

The Chinese Calendar

Evidence from the Shang oracle bone inscriptions shows that as early as the fourteenth century BC, the Shang Chinese had established the solar year at 365¼ days and lunations (the time between new moons) at 29½ days. The ancient Chinese calendar was lunisolar and the ordinary year contained twelve lunar months. As this was shorter than the solar year, in seven years out of every nineteen a thirteenth intercalary month was inserted during the year to bring the calendar back in step with the seasons. Because of this, and the need for accurate dates for agriculture, there was an underlying solar year which was divided into 24 sections. These have colourful names such as the Waking of Insects, Grain in the Ear and White Dew. Although most festivals are fixed by the lunar calendar some, such as Qingming, are fixed in the solar cycle.

The Chinese new year begins with the first new moon after the sun enters Aquarius, that is the second new moon after the winter solstice. Thus New Year's Day falls any time between January 21 and February 20.

The years in the Chinese calendar are named after twelve animals which follow one another in rotation. According to one form of the legend, these animals quarrelled one day as to who was to head the cycle of years. When asked to decide, the gods suggested a contest. Whoever was to reach the bank of a certain river first would head the cycle, and the rest of the animals would be grouped accordingly. All the animals assembled at the river and the ox plunged in. Unknown to him, the rat jumped on his back. Just before the ox reached the bank, the rat jumped off his back and stepped ashore. Thus the cycle starts with the rat.

The animals in order, with their Chinese names are:

Shu	Rat
Niu	Ox
Hu	Tiger
Tu	Hare
Long	Dragon
She	Snake
Ma	Horse
Yang	Goat
Hou	Monkey
Ji	Cock
Gou	Dog
Zhu	Pig

Chinese horoscopes are based on the characteristics of the animal sign for the year of a person's birth, rather than on the month as for Western horoscopes. All Chinese know their animal sign, and from it one can easily guess a person's age (to a multiple of twelve years).

Nowadays in China and Hong Kong the Western calendar is used for all administrative purposes, but the lunar calendar is still popularly used for most festivals, religious activities and birthdays.

The Baha'i Calendar

The Baha'i Era dates from 1844. The calendar year consists of nineteen months each of nineteen days duration, adding up to 361 days, with four intercalary days between the eighteenth and nineteenth months. The leap year has five intercalary days.

The names of the nineteen months represent various sublime attributes, and the avoidance of references to old pagan feasts and Roman holidays emphasises the arrival of a new era. The months are:

Month	Arabic Name	Translation	First days
1	Bahá	Splendour	21 March
2	Jalál	Glory	9 April
3	Jamál	Beauty	28 April
4	'Azamat	Grandeur	17 May
5	Núr	Light	5 June
6	Rahmet	Mercy	24 June
7	Kalimát	Words	13 July

8	Kamál	Perfection	1 August
9	Asmá'	Names	20 August
10	'Izzat	Might	8 September
11	Mashíyyat	Will	27 September
12	'Ilm	Knowledge	16 October
13	Quadrat	Power	4 November
14	Qawl	Speech	23 November
15	Masá'il	Questions	12 December
16	Sharaf	Honour	31 December
17	Sultan	Sovereignty	19 January
18	Mulk	Dominion	7 February
19	'Alá	Loftiness	2 March

The cycle of the year ends with nineteen days of fasting to prepare for the coming of the New Year (Naw-Ruz). The Baha'i day starts and ends at sunset. The dates of the celebration of feasts are adjusted to conform to the Baha'i calendar time.

The important anniversaries and festivals observed by the Baha'is are:

Festival of Ridvan (Declaration of Baha'u'llah)	21 April – 2 May 1863
Declaration of the Bab	23 May
Ascension of Baha'u'llah	29 May
Martyrdom of the Bab	9 July
Birth of the Bab	20 October
Birth of Baha'u'llah	12 November
Day of the Covenant	26 November
Ascension of Abdu'l-Baha	28 November
Period of the fast	19 days beginning 2 March
Feast of Naw-Ruz (Baha'i New Year)	21 March*

According to Baha'i laws, work is forbidden on Nine Holy Days. These are:

The first day of Ridvan	The anniversary of the declaration of the Bab
The ninth day of Ridvan	The anniversary of the birth of Baha'u'llah
The twelfth day of Ridvan	The anniversary of the birth of the Bab
The feast of Naw-Ruz	The anniversary of the ascension of Baha'u'llah
	The anniversary of the martyrdom of the Bab

*If the vernal equinox falls on 21 March before sunset, Naw-Ruz is celebrated on that day. If at any time after sunset, the New Year will then fall on 22 March.

Origins and Beliefs of the Major Religions, Festivals and High Holy Days

For a great many people, religion is woven into the fabric of society and life. It is something 'done' and lived rather than a cerebral activity. Festival rituals and celebrations are frequently the mode in which fundamental religious beliefs and values are expressed and reinforced. A succinct account of the main living religions of the world is presented as a background for the feasts and festivals described.

Hinduism

Hinduism is one of the world's oldest living faiths in which complex rituals and practices co-exist with highly philosophical and metaphysical systems. Attempts to define Hinduism encounter innumerable difficulties since there is no single founder or book which is acknowledged by all Hindus as being the source of their faith. The classical Hindu language, Sanskrit, has no exact equivalent for the word 'Religion'. Hindus themselves refer to their faith as 'Sanatana dharma' or eternal law.

Hindu religious belief begins with the assumption that all living things have a soul which passes through successive cycles of birth and rebirth. The main preoccupation of the religious-minded has been to transcend this cycle through closer identification with the undifferentiated source of the universe – the Brahman.

In its higher manifestations, Hinduism is essentially monotheistic since all differences are reduced to a single entity – the Brahman. At the level of popular Hindusim, however, there is a multiplicity of deities and divinities, each of whom has been attributed distinctive characteristics and special powers.

The power regarded in the ancient Hindu texts, the Upanishads, as being universal and the elemental matter from which everything originated, became personalised under the name of **Brahma.** In later texts, including the great Hindu epic, the Mahabharata, Brahma was closely associated with the origin and control of the universe. From the 6th century AD onwards, however, the worship of Brahma gradually declined and there are few temples dedicated to this god.

According to the Hindu world view, the world passes through cycles of creation which are related to the life of the god **Vishnu.**

As the preserver of the universe, Vishnu is believed to have descended to the world in various forms and guises to restore righteousness. Hindus believe that there have been nine full incarnations of Vishnu so far, with one more yet to come. The seventh and eighth incarnations as **Rama** and **Krishna** have great religious significance for it is in these forms that Vishnu is chiefly worshipped by Hindus.

Rama is the hero of the great Hindu epic, the 'Ramayana' and epitomises honour, filial piety and nobility of character. His victory over the demon-king Ravana is celebrated in the Hindu festival of Dassera and his triumphant return to his capital after fourteen years in exile is one of the legends associated with the festival of 'Diwali'.

As Hinduism developed, its followers branched out into two main sects – those who focused their spiritual attention on Vishnu (Vaishnavites), and those who focused on **Siva** (the Saivites). The divisions are not entirely clear cut; neither are the beliefs and devotional practices of the two sects mutually exclusive.

While Vishnu is conceived of as a benevolent creator, Siva combines the powers of creation, preservation and destruction. The festival of Sivaratri is celebrated by Hindus of all castes in honour of this god.

One of the most popular deities in the Hindu pantheon is Siva's son **Ganesha,** the elephant-headed god. Also known as **Vighneshwara** the remover of all obstacles, he is propitiated by Hindus before the commencement of any ritual or enterprise.

Goddess worship has long been a significant aspect of Hinduism. In fact, no other living religious tradition has displayed such an ancient, continuous and diverse history of goddess worship. Each of the female deities, such as Parvati, Lakshmi, Durga and Saraswati has a coherent mythology, theology and in some cases, a cult of her own. During the nine-day festival of Dassera, Hindus worship the goddess Kali (who is associated with death and destruction as well as creation and fertility), Lakshmi (the goddess of wealth, beauty and good fortune) and Saraswati (the goddess of wisdom and learning).

Hanuman the monkey god, is another popular deity and there are many temples in India dedicated to him. He is believed to have helped **Rama** in his war against **Ravana** and for Hindus he epitomises devotion and loyalty. In many temples special prayers are offered to Hanuman on Tuesdays and Saturdays.

Hindu Festivals

All Hindu festivals have a deep spiritual import, besides commemorating certain historical and mythological events. Since most festivals are based on the lunar calendar, the dates vary from year to year. Traditional ways of celebrating them also vary in different parts of India, among expatriate Indian communities and between different sects and castes. Festivals may be celebrated in the home, in the presence of the family deities, or by the worshipping community, congregated in a temple.

The Hindu temple is conceptualised as the palace of a king and temple worship resembles the hospitality accorded a royal personage. Hindu 'puja' or ritual consists of specific actions which represent the invocation, reception and entertainment of a god as a royal guest. The religious ceremony is completed by the 'arati' or the waving of burning lights in front of the image of the deity, which is then passed among the worshippers as an act of purification and sanctification.

On festival days, temple rituals commence with the elaborate ritual cleansing of the image of the deity who is the particular focus of worship on that day, with recitations from the sacred texts and congregational singing. In the home, the festival may be observed by the ceremonial cleansing of the house, decorating the entrance with pictures and patterns drawn with coloured powder **(rangoli)**, an elaborate feast, the exchange of gifts, and fireworks. Certain festivals are also marked in a more austere manner, by fasting and spending time in prayer and meditation.

Lohri

Lohri is the winter festival of the Punjab and is celebrated by Hindus and Sikhs (see page 56).

Makara Sankrant

Makara Sankrant is observed by Hindus all over India as the Winter Solstice Festival. The day is spent in prayer and in the State of Maharashtra, a special sweet made of sesame seeds (symbolising life) is distributed to friends and relatives.

Pongal

Hindus in the southern Indian states of Tamil Nadu, Andhra Pradesh and Karnataka celebrate the Pongal-Sankranti festival to coincide with the winter solstice or the sun's entry into the sign of Capricorn. It is an important harvest festival and the celebrations extend over three days.

The first day is called Bhogi Pongal and is observed as a family feast. The main feature of the second day's celebrations is the worship of Surya or the sun god. The third day, Mathu Pongal, is the most important and is observed as the day for the worship of cattle. Cows and oxen are bathed and decorated with garlands of flowers and worshipped. Pongal, a sweet made of rice, is offered to the household deity and then distributed to family members as well as given to the cattle to eat.

Vasanta Panchami

The festival of Vasanta Panchami is enthusiastically celebrated by all Hindus in the month of Magha (January–February), mainly in honour of Saraswati, the goddess of learning, wisdom and fine arts.

Saraswati is an exceptionally charming goddess who plays on the musical instrument 'vina'. Her mount is a white swan. In every part of India, Hindu children start their education by writing the alphabet in front of the image of Saraswati. She bestows every success on her worshippers, and without her grace none can attain proficiency in poetry, music or fine arts. Saraswati is mainly a deity for personal worship rather than community adoration. The worship of Saraswati is particularly popular in Bengal.

Mahasivaratri

Mahasivaratri is celebrated by Hindus in honour of the marriage of Lord Siva to Parvati. Devotees observe a strict fast on this day and keep vigil all night. Congregational worship in Hindu temples consists of hymns in praise of Lord Siva and sacred chanting.

The festival normally falls on the thirteenth or fourteenth day of the month of Phalguna (February–March) in the Hindu calendar.

Holi

Holi is the most colourful of Hindu festivals. It is a spring festival celebrated on the full moon day of the month of Phalguna (February–March). It falls when the season is neither hot nor cold and the trees bloom with different kinds of flowers.

According to legend, a mighty king named Hiranya Kashipu once ruled on the earth. His arrogance grew to such an extent that he declared himself to be a god and ordered his people to worship him. But Prahlad, the king's only son, refused to accept him as a god, as he had firm belief only in Rama. To punish his son, the King took different severe measures and even tried to kill him, but all the time Prahlad was saved as he uttered the name of Vishnu. At last, Prahlad's aunt, Holika, claiming that she was fireproof, took the child in her lap and sat in the fire to burn him alive. When the flames died down, the King found the child was safe but his aunt had perished in the fire.

Another legend associated with Holi is about the destruction of the handsome Kama, the god of love, by Shiva. In south India, the songs sung during Holi include the lamentations of Rati, Kama's wife.

According to another account, the festival of Holi was instituted to commemorate the destruction by Krishna of a female demon called Putana. When Krishna was a baby, his uncle Kansa, who was his enemy and the King of Mathura, ordered a general massacre of all children in order to destroy him. One of Kansa's agents was a female fiend named Putana, who assumed human form and went about the country sucking to death every child she found; but the infant Krishna, knowing her to be a fiend, sucked her blood and thus destroyed her. Those who attribute the origin of all festivals to seasonal cycles maintain that Putana represents winter and her death and cremation, the cessation of winter.

The festival takes two days for its observance. On the first day, a bonfire is lit either in the evening or during the night. The effigy of Holika is placed in the centre of the pile and a ministering brahmin recites verses in the worship of Holi before setting it on fire. People then return to their homes.

On the second day, from early morning till noon, people, irrespective of caste and creed, amuse themselves by throwing handfuls of coloured powder on their friends and relatives; or they spray coloured water with sprayers. The damage to people's clothes is taken in good spirit. The same evening, people exchange sweetmeats and friends embrace and wish each other good luck. The children and the young touch the feet of their elders to express their reverence.

Ramnavami

The festival of Ramnavami is celebrated throughout India to commemorate the birth of Shri Rama, who was born to King Dasharatha of Ayodhya on the ninth lunar day in the bright fortnight of Chaitra (March–April). It is observed with sanctity and fasting. On this day, temples are decorated, religious discourses are held, and the 'Ramayana' (the life story of Rama) is recited in most Hindu homes. Thousands of devotees throng to temples to have 'darshana' (visualisation of the deity) of the beautiful images of Rama enshrined there.

Vishu – The Malayalam New Year

Vishu is celebrated by Hindus in Kerala (a state in south-west India) as the New Year. This festival coincides with spring and the beginning of the zodiacal cycle when the sun enters the sign of Aries.

Preparations for this festival start the day before, when the house is cleaned and an artistic arrangement of beautiful and auspicious objects is created in the room (or area) where the family deities are enshrined. The items used in this arrangement include flowers (especially yellow laburnums), fruit (especially the yellow citrus variety), vegetables such as pumpkins, coconuts, rice, polished brass and bronze lamps, a small mirror, a gold ornament and silver coins.

Children do not participate in the preparations and are generally not allowed to see the display until the next day, when they are awakened at dawn and led with their eyes closed to the 'puja' room. Thus, the first sight to greet their eyes on New Year's Day is this beautiful arrangement. They are then presented with new clothes and gifts of money.

A feast, to which friends and relatives are invited, is an essential element in the day's festivities.

Rakshabandhan

The Rakshabandhan festival is celebrated especially in northern India in the month of Sravana (July–August). The word Raksha signifies protection. The festival is also called Saluno.

Girls and married women tie a rakhi, made of twisted golden or simple yellow threads, on the right wrist of their brothers, for their welfare and also for protection from any evil influence, and in return they receive cash and gifts. This is an age-old festival, which strengthens the bond of love between brothers and sisters.

On this day, members of a Hindu family bathe very early and go to market to purchase rakhi and sweets from the colourful stalls, which spring up everywhere. The men, dressed in their best, and women in their bright costumes, first offer a prayer to their daily deity. A man considers it a privilege to be chosen as a brother by a girl who ties a rakhi on his wrist. If the brother is not at hand, the rakhi is sent to him by post or passed on to him by someone. In some parts of India, women also tie rakhies to close friends and neighbours.

The brahmins, or the priestly class, also tie rakhi to their 'yajamanas', (patrons and clients), recite hymns for their safety and receive something in cash or kind from them.

The rakhi festival has a special appeal in India which extends to other non-Hindu communities. One story tells of how, during the Muslim rule, a beautiful Hindu queen called Padmini sought protection from the Mughal Emperor by sending him a rakhi. When Padmini was threatened by another Muslim king who had determined to marry her when he saw her reflection in the mirror, the Queen was defended against his invasion by the Mughal Emperor in response to the rakhi. To this day, rakhi from a woman is honoured even when the man is not a Hindu.

Janmashtami

The popular festival of Janmashtami is observed throughout India at midnight, on the night of the new moon during the month of Bhadrapada (August–September). It is joyously celebrated in honour of Lord Krishna, who was born on this day, at Mathura in Uttar Pradesh.

On the festival day, all temples and many

Hindu homes are beautifully and tastefully decorated to welcome the birth of divine chief, Krishna. His image is placed on a swing, in a decorated 'mandapa' (small pavilion). Every member of the family, including children, observes a fast for the whole day and only breaks it when the moon is visible at midnight, at which time the small image of a crawling Krishna is first bathed in 'charnamrita' (curd mixed with milk, dry fruits and leaves of the 'tulsi' plant) and then the 'arati' is performed. (Arati is the veneration and supplication accompanied by circular movements of the lamp and by the throwing of flower petals.) The 'prasada' is distributed to all present and thus the day-long fast is broken. (Prasada is symbolic communion in food and is usually made of semolina, sugar and water.)

Ganesh Chaturthi

Ganesha, the elephant-headed god in the Hindu pantheon, is worshipped all over India as the remover of obstacles. His blessings are especially invoked before the start of any important enterprise. On this day, prayers are offered to the god along with specially prepared foods.

In the city of Bombay and in other parts of the State of Maharashtra, this festival has always been closely associated with a strong feeling of nationalism and is celebrated in a particularly dramatic manner. Gaily coloured and garlanded statues of the god are taken out in procession through city streets and are finally immersed in the sea to the accompaniment of loud chantings and music.

'Prasada' is then distributed to the gathering of devotees.

In parts of southern India, devotees of Ganesha believe that it is unlucky and inauspicious to look at the moon on this day. The belief has its origins in a myth referring to the god and his love of good food, especially 'laddus' (sweetmeats) and coconut. Thus, it is said, that when Ganesha was returning from a celestial banquet, he saw a reflection of the new moon in a pool of water. Mistaking it for a sliver of coconut, he stooped down from his mouse-drawn carriage to pick it up. Seeing this, the moon laughed loudly and Ganesha, highly offended, cursed her and all those who saw her on this day.

Dassera

Dassera, one of the most popular festivals in India, is celebrated all over the country for ten days in the month of Asvina (September–October). The festival, besides other minor functions, comprises the worship of the goddess Durga, during Navaratri (Nine Nights), the 'Ram-Lila', 'Vijayadasmi' and Maha Ashtami.

Among the Hindu festivals, Durga Puja is unique. The festival starts on the first night of the Hindu month of Asvina. Durga is worshipped as Divine Mother or as Kumari, the virgin goddess. The Saktas, who consider the goddess as the supreme deity, worship a manifestation of the goddess on each of the Navaratri nights. Usually, the images of the goddess are installed in people's homes or, in the case of community worship, in public places, and worshipped by the performance of puja (worship), by katha and religious music. Katha is storytelling, and it is a favourite exercise in devotion among Hindus. A pandit, well versed in ancient lore, reads passages from a text extolling the deity. He explains it to the audience with comments enlivened by many anecdotes and tales.

In the Punjab, the first seven nights of Navaratri are considered a period of fast. According to a legend, malicious demons who ruled the Punjab forbade the people from eating anything, all the available food being consumed by the voracious brood. On this day, the people prayed to the goddess Durga who appeared in her war-like form and fought the demons for seven days and put them to flight. On the eighth, the goddess went among the people and asked them to feast themselves. In memory of this, the people of Punjab observe the first seven days of Navaratri as a period of austerity, but on the eighth, ample amends are made by feasting.

In Gujerat, the celebration of Navaratri, or Nine Nights, is marked by 'Garba', a dance performed by women. They joyfully dance around an earthern lamp placed on a stand, singing and clapping hands in rhythmic movements. In Tamil Nadu, the first three days of the festival are dedicated to the goddess Durga, the next three days to the goddess Lakshmi and the last three days to the goddess Saraswati. Durga worship is especially popular in Bengal. Both Hindus and non-Hindus worship her in the form of Kali.

After nine nights (Navaratri) of fasting and worship, the images of Durga are taken out in procession and immersed in a tank, river or in the sea.

The main feature of Dassera, especially in Northern India, is the Ram-Lila based on the epic story of Ramayana. During this week, dramatic troupes perform plays based on the Ramayana.

On Vijaya-dasmi Day, which is the last day of the Dassera festival, the worship of gods, especially Lord Rama, is done with fervour, and prayers are offered in every home. Poor people and the brahmins carrying navatras (small fresh offshoots of barley plants, which are sown in every house on the first day of the festival), go to wealthy people to offer them stalks of navatras and receive alms in return.

Though celebrated all over India by common folk, Dassera is chiefly a royal festival beloved of the ruling classes. With independence and the disappearance of the princes from the Indian political scene, these ancient pageants are dying out and the festival is becoming more democratic than regal. However, it is still considered of great importance by the displaced rulers.

Karva Chauth

According to legend, a princess observed a fast for a whole day. When she broke the fast at dusk, she received news about her husband's death. As she made her way to her husband's dead body, Parvati, the consort of the Lord Siva, met her and blessed her. She gave the princess some blood out of her finger with which she was asked to annoint her dead husband. The man immediately sprang to life. Hence, on this day, married women observe a fast for the whole day, for the welfare, prosperity and longevity of their husbands.

Prayers are offered to the god Siva and his consort, Parvati. At dusk upon sighting the moon, water and flowers are offered to the household deity. An elderly woman usually recites the story of Karva Chauth and the fast is broken.

On this occasion, mothers bless their married daughters and present them with jewellery, garments and sweetmeats.

Diwali (Deepawali)

Diwali or Deepawali is the festival of lights. It is celebrated on the new moon day (Amavasya) of the month of Karthika in the Hindu calendar, and generally falls sometime in late October/early November. It is a five-day festival which includes the last two days of the month of Asvina and the first three days of Karthika.

As with most Hindu festivals, Deepawali has great religious significance. The celebrations consist of prayers and meditations upon Lakshmi (the goddess of prosperity), her consort Vishnu, Durga (the goddess of primal energy – Sakti) and her consort Siva and Saraswati (the goddess of learning). Rama and Krishna, incarnations of Vishnu are also worshipped during this festival.

Hindus associate the five-day festival with a number of historical and religious events. 'Dhan Trayodashi' is the day to buy new clothes and gifts to commence the festivities. The Puranic story associated with the celebrations on this day is that of the legendary churning of the ocean for 'amrit' the life-giving elixir, by the gods and the demons. Dhanvantary, the god of health, is believed to have emerged from the ocean bearing the pot containing the 'amrit' on this day.

On 'Narak Chaturdashi', Krishna is worshipped. According to popular belief in Gujerat and the west coast of India, Krishna killed the demon Narakasura on this day and liberated several thousand innocent women prisoners.

On 'Mahalakshmi Amavasya', businessmen offer prayers and dedicate their account books to the goddess Lakshmi. According to a legend which has wide currency, Lakshmi promised to visit and bless those houses where she is welcomed by lights.

'Govardhan Anakuta' is the day to worship Krishna who is believed to have saved thousands of cows and cowherds from torrential rains by lifting Mount Govardhana and holding it over them like a giant umbrella.

On 'Bhratri Dwitiya', sisters remind their brothers of their pledge to protect them from any danger. Girls and women tie a cotton thread on the right wrist of their brothers, followed by the application of a 'tilak' or red mark on their forehead and the offering of sweets. Brothers, in turn, give gifts of jewellery, clothes or money to their sisters.

Deepawali is also celebrated as the coronation day of Lord Rama who after fourteen years of exile – and vanquishing the demon king, Ravana – returned in triumph to his capital, Ayodhya. It is also associated with the coronation of the Emperor Vikramaditya who started the new Hindu Era – the Vikram Samvat.

Deepawali is a harvest festival and marks the end of the monsoon season and the beginning of winter. Houses are cleaned and decorated, lit with candles and small oil lamps (diva). Gifts and sweets are exchanged among friends and relatives and businessmen open their account books for the new year.

There is a pervading spirit of joy and happiness to mark the beginning of the new year, and the triumph of good over evil.

Islam

The word 'Islam' is derived from the Arabic verb **'aslama'** which means 'to submit' and it denotes the characteristic attitude of the true believer in relation to God. The followers of Islam are called Muslims. A true Muslim, by definition, is one who has submitted to the will of God. Islamic beliefs and practices are based upon the **Holy Quran.** Muslims regard it as the infallible, incontrovertible message of God (**Allah**) to mankind, as revealed to his Prophet Mohammed.

Islam does not recognise the concept of a Church and its theologians and religious scholars do not enjoy the status of a priesthood. Each individual is expected to create a direct link to God without the help of intermediaries. There are five essential Islamic practices, known as the Pillars of the Faith.

The First Pillar: The Profession of Faith (Shahada): The essence of being a Muslim is to recite with sincere 'intention' the simple Islamic creed – "There is no God but the One God; and Mohammed is the Messenger of God."

The Second Pillar: Worship (Salat): Every Muslim is obliged to perform the ritual of prayer at the five prescribed times of dawn, mid-day, afternoon, sunset and night.

Before commencing the act of worship, the individual is required to cleanse the face, head, arms, feet and ankles. The daily prayers may be performed at home or congregationally in a mosque. The noon prayer on Friday is the principal congregational service of the week.

The Third Pillar: Almsgiving (Zakat): From its very early beginnings, Islam emphasised the moral obligation of sharing one's wealth with the less fortunate sections of the worshipping community. In some Islamic countries, **'Zakat'** is levied by the State. Elsewhere, however, almsgiving has become a voluntary practice.

The Fourth Pillar: Fasting (Sawm): The Quran makes it obligatory for all devout Muslims to fast during the hours of daylight throughout the holy month of **Ramadhan** – the ninth month in the Islamic lunar calendar during which the Quran was revealed to the Prophet Mohammed.

The month of Ramadhan is a period of repentance and heightened devotion. The night of **Lailat-ul-Quadr** – 27th of Ramadhan, which commemorates the revelation of the Holy Quran is considered to be a particularly significant event in the Islamic ritual calendar and an appropriate time for an act of devotion.

The month-long period of fasting culminates in the festival of **Eid-ul-Fitr.**

The Fifth Pillar: The Pilgrimage (Haj): At least once in their lifetime, provided that they have the means to do so, Muslims are expected to undertake a pilgrimage to the sacred mosques at Mecca and its vicinity. The profoundly spiritual experience as well as the sense of community heightened by participation in joint rituals and congregational worship, give the pilgrimage its special significance within the Islamic tradition.

Muslim Festivals

For Muslims, all religious festivals have a special significance. At the end of different modes of worship, Islam has instituted a festival. Thus, for instance, the daily prayers of the week culminate in the festival of the Friday Prayer, called **Juma Prayer.** The festival following the month of fasting is called **Eid-ul-Fitr,** while that following the ceremony of Haj is known as **Eid-ul-Adha.**

Festivals are not merely occasions of joy and happiness. They are also a form of worship in themselves, as Islam grafts the remembrance of God with every activity of a Muslim, even sitting, walking, sleeping, wearing shoes or garments, going in or out of the house, setting out on a journey or returning from one, selling or buying, eating, drinking, washing, bathing, entering or leaving a mosque, meeting a friend or facing an enemy, seeing the moon, starting any work or finishing it, even sneezing, yawning or taking medicine.

The day of a festival is spent in praising Allah, remembering his attributes and thanking Him for his countless bounties, as well as in merry-making. Islam, however, forbids its followers from indulging in extravagance at any time. The faithful are exhorted not to go to extremes so as to stand on the brink of insanity, either with excessive joy or with grief and sorrow. Followers of the religion are also instructed by the Holy Quran to share their happiness with others, especially the poor and the needy.

'Children of Adam, put your minds and bodies in a state of tidiness at every time and place of worship and eat and drink but be not wasteful; surely, he does not love the wasteful.

(The Holy Quran 7:32)

Islamic festivals are based on lunar sightings rather than lunar reckonings.

Hijrat – Muslim New Year

This is celebrated on the first of Muharram. Hijrat means leaving one place of residence for another. In the history of Islam, it happened when the Holy Prophet of Islam migrated from Mecca, where he and his followers were persecuted, to Medina where they were welcomed by the populace in AD 622. This event is known as Hijrat. The first mosque was built at Medina and the Islamic social order and code of practice established.

Muharram

Muharram is the name of the first month of the Muslim year. The first day of Muharram is declared a public holiday in Muslim countries. The Muslim calendar dates from the year the Prophet Mohammed – under pressure of persecution from the Mecca unbelievers – accepted the believers' invitation and emigrated to Medina in AD 622. The first ten days commemorate the loss of many prominent members of the Prophet's family and a number of his followers, when they were surrounded by the force of Yazid, the Muslim ruler of that time, while they were on a journey. They were deprived of food and water and many of them were put to death. The incident happened at a place called Karbala in Iraq, in the 61st year of the Hijira (AH 61). After the death of the fourth Caliph (Hasrat Ali), Muslims were divided in their opinion as to whom should be their new Caliph. As a result they fought with one another and there was a lot of bloodshed.

The tenth of Muharram is a festival called Ashuraa and is especially remembered by the Shia sect as they observe this festival after Imam Hussain.

Ashuraa – Tenth Day of Muharram

Some Muslim sects observe this festival with great respect, through prayers, talks and vigils, and singing dirges in memory of Imam Hussain, the grandson of Prophet Mohammed. It commemorates the great tragedy at Karbala at Mecca in which Imam Hussain was brutally speared to death in the sixty-first year of the Hijira (AH), and when practically all of the Prophet's family including his son-in-law, Hazrat Ali, were annihilated.

Members of the Shia sect dress in black

clothes as they spend the first ten days of the year in mourning. Assemblies are held every day for the first nine days, where Shia orators relate the incident of the death of Imam Hussain and his party in great detail. On the Tenth Day of Muharram, large processions are formed and the devoted followers parade the streets holding banners and carrying models of the mausoleum of Imam Hussain and his people who fell at Karbala. They show their grief and sorrow by inflicting wounds on their own bodies with sharp metal pieces tied to a chain with which they scourge themselves, to depict the sufferings of the martyrs. It is a sad occasion and everyone in the procession chants "Ya Hussain," with loud wails of lamentation. Usually, a white horse, beautifully decorated for the occasion, is also included in the procession, perhaps to mark the empty mount of Imam Hussain after his martyrdom.

During these ten days, drinking posts are also set up temporarily by the Shia community where water and fruit juices are served to all, free of charge. It has also become customary to serve milk, or 'sharbat' (soft drinks) at these functions to remind Muslims of the way Imam Hussain and his followers were starved and tortured to death.

On this day, God saved Moses and his followers from the pursuing army of the self-appointed god, Pharoah. The Prophet asked his followers to honour this occasion by fasting.

Eid Milad-un-Nabi

This festival commemorates the anniversary of the birth of the Holy Prophet Mohammed. It is celebrated on the twelfth day of Rabee-ul-Awwal. From the point of view of Muslims, this date marks the most important event in the history of the world. Mohammed is regarded as the last and the chief of the Prophets, the perfect man to whom the Holy Quran was revealed, the best example, and the greatest benefactor of mankind. He is the person for whom God has proclaimed:

'Allah sends down his blessings on the Prophet, and his angels constantly invoke his blessings on him, do you O believers, also invoke Allah's blessings on him and offer him the salutation of peace.'
(The Holy Quran 33:57)

The extent of festivities, on this occasion, is however restricted because the same day also marks the anniversary of his death.

On this occasion, therefore, public meetings are held in the mosques, where religious leaders make speeches on different aspects of the life of this great man. The stories of the Prophet's birth, childhood, youth and manhood, character, teachings, sufferings and forgiveness of even his most bitter enemies, his fortitude in the face of general opposition, leadership in battles, bravery, wisdom, preachings and his final triumph through God's mercy over the hearts of the people, are narrated in detail.

Salutations and songs in his praise are sung. In some countries, streets, mosques and public buildings are decorated with colourful bunting and pennants and are well illuminated at night.

Devout Muslims give large sums of money to charity. Feasts are arranged and rice and meat dishes are served to the guests and also distributed among the poor. In some big cities, large processions are also formed, and people in jubilant mood chant verses in praise of the Holy Prophet Mohammed.

Some Muslims, however, do not celebrate this occasion as his birthday or death anniversaries as they believe such celebrations are not part of Muslim society as such. Instead they hold Seer-un-Nabi meetings where speeches are made on different aspects of the life of the Prophet.

Shab-e-Miraj

Shab-e-Miraj means the night of the ascent. It is a blessed night when the Holy Prophet of Islam was spiritually transported to heaven and reached such a high stage of nearness to God Almighty as was beyond human mind to conceive. The ascent took place in the fifth year of the call, about seven years before Hijrat. The journey was with a vision of the highest type. On the way to meeting God, the Holy Prophet met Adam, Abraham, Moses, Jesus and some other prophets. The purpose of this spiritual ascent was to confirm the status of the Prophet of Islam, a position which all Muslims believe is impossible to attain by any other human being. It is related that even Gabriel, the Angel who was accompanying the Prophet, remarked at one stage, "I am forced to stop here. I cannot go any further but you, O Messenger of Peace and friend of the Master of the World, continue your glorious ascent."

It is also related that the Holy Prophet continued his journey until he was very close to the throne of God and attained the utmost nearness to him. After having drunk fully at the divine fountain of spiritual knowledge, he came down to impart that knowledge to mankind.

According to popular belief Miraj, or spiritual ascension, took place on the twenty-seventh day of Rajab. Muslims celebrate the occasion by holding prayers and reminding themselves of the high morals taught during this night's journey. In some Muslim countries, the houses, streets and especially the mosques are decorated with colourful pennants and bunting, and at night, they are well illuminated by means of electric lights, candles or even oil lamps. In the evening, worshippers assemble in the mosques, and there often is a speaker to address the pious crowd at this holy event. After the ceremony is over, sweets are distributed to all. Most of this holy night is spent in prayer, and many wealthy Muslims share some of their wealth by distributing money and food amongst the poor and destitute.

Shab-e-Barat

This day falls about a fortnight before Ramadhan, and is traditionally celebrated in anticipation and preparation for the month of Ramadhan. Muslims fast and spend the night in prayer, as God is said to make a record of all the good and bad actions of man and to dispose their fate according to their actions.

Originally intended by the Prophet of Islam as an occasion for vigils and fasting, this has developed into a joyous festival celebrated in many parts of the world, when sweets, halva (sweetmeats made of sesame seeds and honey) and bread are specially prepared and distributed to friends and to the poor.

Ramadhan

Fasting is one of the five pillars of Islam, and the month of Ramadhan is the ninth month of the Muslim calendar, which the Prophet Mohammed chose to be spent restfully in prayer and meditation.

Muslims do not worship Mohammed, but they do regard him as the greatest Prophet of God, as he was the last to descend to earth and he was the one who actually completed the message left by former prophets. The encounter with the Angels is reserved only for the chosen ones and the messengers of God. They received their messages mainly through the Archangel Gabriel, who is described as powerful and honest, and is named in the Quran as the Holy Spirit who carried God's messages to His blessed prophets including Noah, Ibrahim, Lot, Ismail, Ishak, Yakoub, Yousuf, Musa (Moses), Haroun, El-Azer, Zakariya, Yahya (John) and Isa (Jesus).

Ramadhan is a very special month, as it is the month in which the Quran was first revealed as God's guidance to mankind. To mark their celebration and their gratitude, Muslims sacrifice some of their daytime material pleasures as an offering to the merciful God.

It is the sacrificial abstention from the material pleasures of food and water from dawn to sunset, while abstaining in the meantime from evil deeds. Fasting enables the rich to enter the experience of poverty and to teach the value of self discipline.

The Quran states:

'O ye who believe fasting is prescribed for you as it was prescribed for those before you, so that you may guard against evil.'
(2:184)

The fast is obligatory for every healthy, adult Muslim, male or female, but there are certain exemptions: for a sick person, a person who is travelling, a pregnant woman or one who is breastfeeding her child, and those who find the severity of the fast hard to bear on account of age or other infirmity. When the reason for exemption is only temporary, as with an illness from which the person recovers, the number of days missed are later made up. Should the cause of exemption continue over a lengthy period of time or become permanent, as in the case of the infirm and elderly, the exemption is absolute, but the person concerned, if he can afford to, should arrange to provide food for a poor person for the whole month or give the equivalent amount in charity known as fidya.

Fasting during this month is to make man realise his many blessings and is a means of showing his thanksgiving and gratitude to God.

While the reward for every good action is prescribed by God and is written down by the recording angels, the reward for fasting is awarded and recorded by God himself. It is a month of communal worship when the Quran is read often, as it is believed that it was revealed around the twenty-seventh day of Ramadhan.

Lailat-ul-Qadr – Twenty-seventh Ramadhan (The Night of Decrees)

This occasion falls on the eve of the twenty-sixth fast during the month of Ramadhan. It was on this night that the Holy Quran was revealed to the Prophet Mohammed by the Archangel Gabriel, thus it is so important that it is known as 'The Night of Power' which in Arabic is 'Lailat-ul-Qadr'.

The Holy Quran states:

'This month of Ramadhan is the month in which the Quran began to be revealed, the

Book which comprises guidance and divine sign which discriminate between truth and falsehood ...'
(2:186)

Prophet Mohammed was 40 years of age when he first received a revelation in a small cave on Mount Hira, which is a short distance away from Mecca. The Muslims believe that it is during this night that the earth was filled with angels, led by the Archangel Gabriel, to reveal the first verses of the Quran to Mohammed and signal the start of his mission:

'Read in the name of God, who created man from clinging cells, read for your God is the most generous, who taught man with the pen, taught man what he knew not.'

(96:1–5)

It was significant that the first verses called for people to learn God's knowledge, and that it was Mohammed who was chosen to carry the Quran to mankind. The revelation continued until his death, for a period of about 23 years.

The whole month of Ramadhan is a period of spiritual training when believers devote much of their time to fasting, praying and reciting the Holy Quran and remembering God (Allah), as well as giving charity and good will. The last ten nights, especially, are spent in worship and meditation, and the more devout Muslims retreat to the mosque for this time and spend their time solely in the remembrance of Allah. They join the congregation at prayer times and for 'Taraweeh' (special prayers recited with Isha Salat in the evenings).

Devoting their time so fully to the remembrance of Allah, they hope to receive the divine favours and blessings connected with this blessed night. It is related that when the last ten days of Ramadhan began, Mohammed used to stay awake the whole night and was most diligent in worship. Thus Muslims spend this night in remembrance of Allah, asking forgiveness for their shortcomings. They have a firm belief that God accepts the prayers of the supplicant readily during this night.

Jumat-ul-Wida

This is the last Friday of the month in Ramadhan, the holy month of refined celebration, that is eagerly awaited by Muslims and missed when it ends. It is also a month of brotherhood and communal worship, as well as great spirituality, charity, peace and happiness. It is a day that marks the end of Ramadhan and, as a respected visitor, Ramadhan is given a great welcome and likewise a special farewell.

Otherwise, Friday is the Muslim's holy day or Day of Assembly. At midday, Muslims gather at the mosque to pray together and listen to the imam preach his sermon. Work is carried out as normal before and after Friday prayers. Before performing the actual prayer, or handling the Holy Quran, shoes are removed and one performs a Wozoo (holy wash) whereby one cleanses oneself before touching the Holy Quran or doing any pious act. Friday sermons are about Muslims' responsibilities and obligations, and strengthen the spritual bond between the believers.

The Quran says:

'O ye who believe, when the call is made for Prayer on Friday, hasten to the remembrance of God and leave off all business, that is better for you, if you only knew.'

(62:10)

Muslims gather at the mosque to pray together and listen to the imam preach his sermon (khutba) at noon every Friday. But this particular Friday is significant as it is the last Friday of the holy month, and a feeling of both sadness and happiness is experienced, as all the excitement of the month comes to an end, and the people look forward to its return after a year.

Eid-ul-Fitr

Eid is an Arabic word which means a day which returns often. There are two days in the year that are declared public holidays in Muslim countries. One is Eid-ul-Fitr (at the end of Ramadhan) and the other is Eid-ul-Adha which comes about ten weeks after the first Eid.

Eid-ul-Fitr is celebrated at the end of a period of fasting (the holy month of Ramadhan). There is a lot of excitement when the moon is sighted, a joyous surge runs through the hearts of all Muslims, young and old, in anticipation of one of the most joyful Eid festivals. Friends and relations exchange good wishes and blessings with each other. All the necessary preparations are made – shops are opened till late, streets and homes are decorated, and the general preparations for the next day get under way.

The next day, after rising early and having a bath, they wear new clothes (or their best clothes) and a special non-alcoholic perfume called 'athar'. They are treated to a special breakfast which includes a sweet dish of 'sheer-kurma' – vermicelli cooked in milk with dried dates, raisins, almonds and other nuts.

Eagerly they proceed towards the 'Eidgah', which is the central mosque of the city, or to a specified open space that will accommodate the congregation. Separate enclosures are provided for women, because Islam does not permit the free intermingling of men and women. As was the practice of the Holy Prophet Mohammed, they go to the Eidgah generally by one route and return by another.

Eid prayer and Friday prayer is always offered in congregation, but no Adhan or Iqamat (introductory announcement of the prayer or exhortation) is called out for this service.

The prayer commences with the imam calling out "Allah-o-Akbar" (Allah is the Greatest) aloud. When the prayer is over, a sermon is delivered by the imam, which generally includes the historical background and spritual significance of the festival. After the service the worshippers greet each other by saying "Eid Mubarak" and hug each other or just shake hands. The spirit of Eid is one of peace, forgiveness and of brotherhood, so after performing their duty, they return home happy and contented. The women prepare exotic dishes as this is a big day of celebration. They have friends and relations to join them for meals. Gifts and greetings are exchanged. Although it is an occasion for joy and happiness, it is certainly not an occasion to indulge in frivolity, over-eating and mere pursuit of pleasure. The main purpose is always to seek the pleasure of God by glorifying him and rendering thanks to him for having enabled them to perform their duties.

It is a family day in the smaller as well as the wider sense, when Muslims visit friends and relatives to exchange greetings and good wishes. The joy and happiness of the occasion originate mainly from managing to complete the Ramadhan fasting and in being nearer to God.

Haj – Pilgrimage

Haj is one of the five pillars of Islam. Haj is performed during the period from the eighth to thirteenth of Zul-Hijja. During this time pilgrims from all over the globe flock to Mecca in Saudi Arabia, and the finest example of true brotherhood of man is shown to the world, otherwise torn by political, economic, religious and cultural strife. A Muslim makes every effort to perform this pilgrimage at least once in a lifetime, whenever he finds the means to do so.

These are the important rituals associated with the ceremony.

1. Putting on Ihram. A male pilgrim has to discard his usual clothes and dress himself in two white sheets of seamless cloth. One sheet is wrapped round the waist covering the lower abdomen, while the other is slung over the left shoulder. The head remains bare. Women may dress themselves in simple clothes and are not required to cover their faces.

2. Performing seven circuits of the Kaabah, the pilgrims enter the great mosque. The Muslims' spirituality reaches a peak as they leave their worldly cares behind, clothe themselves in simple, humble, white sheets of cloth, and stand, rich and poor, master and servant, shoulder to shoulder, in concentric rings of prayer around the Kaabah, all raising their prayers to the One God who is unseen, but whose presence is felt everywhere. They walk round in an anticlockwise direction, and all say the same phrase that the prophet Abraham said four thousand years ago, which is translated as follows:

'Here I am, my Lord, here I am,
Here I am. There is no associate with thee.
Thine is the kingdom,
There is no associate with thee.'

The Kaabah is a very simple, stone structure, cubic shaped, laying no claim to grandeur of size or beauty of architecture. It impresses by its very simplicity.

3. Performing the Sa'ee, which is going seven times between the two nearby mountains of Safa and Marwah, in commemoration of Hagar, the Egyptian wife of Ibrahim and mother of Ismael, in her attempts to look for water for her thirsty infant Ismael. The pilgrim then goes to drink water from the blessed well of Zam-Zam, that sprang out from underneath the feet of Ismael, in answer to his mother's prayer, and is still flowing to this day.

4. Visiting Mina, Arafat and Muzdalifah. On the eighth of Zul-Hijja, the pilgrims leave Mecca for Mina and spend the night there in prayer and meditation. On the ninth day, they go to Mount Arafat, the 'Mountain of Mercy', where God forgave Adam and Eve and led them back to each other. Being there with a repentant heart on the appointed date is all that is required to earn total forgiveness, yet another example of God's mercy and compassion. They arrive there after midday, offer Zuhr and Asr prayers and remain at Arafat until sunset.

To stay at Arafat from post-meridian until sunset is regarded as an important ritual of Haj, as it is on this plain that man seeks pardon for his sins and returns from Haj as sinless as the day he was born. Pilgrims then proceed to Muzdalifah where Maghrib and Isha prayers are combined and the night is spent in praising God and in meditation. Some small stones are taken from here on the journey back to Mina after the morning prayer the next day. At Mina, the pilgrim stones the three places where Satan appeared to the prophet Abraham, trying to dissuade him from obeying God, as he was on his way to sacrifice his only son, Ismael. The stoning of the three places is to symbolise the Muslims' obedience to God, and their rejection of the Devil.

5. On the tenth day of Zul-Hijja, the pilgrim sacrifices an animal that he can afford, such as a goat, sheep, cow or camel. This is known as the Feast of Sacrifice, thus commemorating the prophet Abraham's success in his test, demonstrating that he loved God more than he loved his son, when God stopped him sacrificing his son and offered him a fat ram to slaughter instead. The purpose of the sacrifice is to feed the poor, as well as one's friends, neighbours and oneself.

6. After staying at Mina for the three days of the feast, the pilgrims return to Mecca for Tawaaf al Widaa, the farewell visit before departure.

7. Pilgrims have their heads shaven or cut their hair short.

Pilgrimage is a time when Islam's history comes alive, especially when one remembers the prophet Mohammed's glorious struggle, resolve, tolerance and wisdom in fulfilling his message. Thus the pilgrims pay their respects by visiting him in the mosque at Medina where he is buried. They return with holy water, dates, and blessings for everybody.

Eid-ul-Adha (Bakra Eid) – The Festival of Sacrifice

The Eid is celebrated with great solemnity and reverence everywhere. As for Eid-ul-Fitr, Muslims make preparations several days before the festival. The animals to be sacrificed are bought well before the Eid day by those who can afford to do so and are well looked after. These animals should be free from all physical defects and should be fully grown. In the case of a sheep or goat, one animal suffices for one household, whereas a cow or camel can be shared by seven.

The details of these events are mentioned in the Bible and in the Quran. It is narrated that Abraham saw a vision that he was slaying his only son Ismael. He mentioned the dream to his son Ismael and asked, "What do you think of it?" Ismael replied, "Father, do that which you have been commanded. You will find me God-willing and steadfast." Being thus convinced that God demanded the sacrifice of his son, who was bestowed to him in his old age, he began to make the necessary preparations. Then Abraham received the revelation that he had indeed fulfilled his covenant, and on God's command, the angels brought a ram instead and put it in place of Ismael. Thus the animal was sacrificed, and this festival of sacrifices therefore urges all Muslims to follow the examples of Abraham, Hagar and Ismael and show perfect submission to God's commands.

Therefore Muslims – especially adults who have performed their pilgrimage – make this sacrifice.

A third of the meat is kept for the use of the household, and the remainder is distributed uncooked among the poor and sent as gifts to friends and relatives.

Many families get together and cook exotic dishes, both savoury and sweet, and rejoice with relations and friends. They wear new clothes and attend prayers at the big mosque called 'Eid Gah'.

Judaism

Judaism has its roots in the Hebrew Bible. This collection of books was written over a period of nearly 1000 years and established in its full canonical form by the end of the first century AD. The Bible is basically a record of the Hebrews' aspirations to understand God and his ways, both in relation to the material world and to humanity.

At the centre of Jewish belief lies the faith in one God, who has made the heaven and the earth and all that they contain, who took the Israelites out of their bondage in Egypt, revealed his divine teaching or **Torah** to them and brought them into the Holy Land.

Prayer is regarded as one of the most solemn and holy observances in Judaism. It is essentially an attempt to realise man's relationship with God and a means to keep open the channels of communication and influence of God upon the worshipper.

The fundamental beliefs of Judaism are expressed through its ritual rather than through abstract doctrine. The Jewish ritual year begins in late September/early October with the New Year festival (Rosh Hashanah).

The Sabbath is considered to be the most important day in the Jewish calendar. It begins each Friday evening at sunset and comes to an end late on Saturday evening. Special rituals mark the beginning and end of the Sabbath, which according to biblical tradition symbolises the original seventh day on which God rested after completing the creation of the universe. Conforming Jews refrain from all kinds of work or secular activity and observe the Sabbath at home and in the synagogue through worship, study and social activities such as visiting friends and relatives.

The Sabbath is welcomed by the women of the house lighting two special candles and saying a blessing over them. This is followed by the **Kiddush,** a blessing pronounced by the male head of household over wine and bread. The family then sit down to the first of three special meals prescribed by tradition as the appropriate number to be eaten on the Sabbath. At the conclusion of the Sabbath, a prayer **(havdalah)** is recited over a cup of wine, over incense and a lighted candle.

Jewish Holy Days and other Festivals

Jewish Holy Days always commence immediately before dusk and terminate at nightfall the following day – a 25-hour period. If there are two consecutive Holy Days, the laws relating to the Festival continue over both days, terminating at nightfall on the second day.

According to Jewish Law 'work' of any sort, including creative activity, travelling, engaging in commercial transactions and operating equipment, even telephones, is strictly prohibited on Holy Days. A 'dispensation' cannot be given by a Rabbi from these restrictions and obligations. However, individuals are free to decide on their own level of observance.

The two most important festivals in the Jewish calendar are **Rosh Hashanah** – the Jewish New Year, and **Yom Kippur** – the Day of Atonement. These High Holy Days are unique because they are the only Jewish festivals which have neither an historical nor an agricultural basis.

Purim

This marks the deliverance of the Jews of Persia from the persecution of Haman, the Prime Minister of King Ahaseurus, and his followers, who planned to exterminate them entirely throughout Persia and its Commonwealth, particularly because Haman hated the wise Jew Mordecai.

Providentially, the tables were turned on him when Mordecai's niece Esther was chosen by King Ahaseurus as his new queen. She pleaded for her people and saved them from destruction.

School may be attended, but the day is usually celebrated with much jollity, including fancy dress.

Pesach or Passover

This celebrates the deliverance of the children of Israel from Egypt where they were held as slaves.

The festival lasts for eight days, during which no bread, cakes or similar foodstuffs may be eaten, and on Matzoth unleavened bread is substituted for these.

The first two and last two days are particularly holy, and Jewish children do not attend school on these days.

On the eve of the first two days, special celebrations, called the Seder, are held in

Jewish homes when families gather together for a festival meal preceded by recounting the story of the exodus from Egypt.

Lag B'Omer

On the second day of Passover in ancient Israel, the first sheaf was cut of the barley harvest and offered up in the Temple. This started the counting of the Omer (a measure of the grain) leading to Shavuot. The Jewish people were commanded to count the days during these seven weeks.

During this period there was plague among numerous pupils of the great Mishnaic scholar, Rabbi Akiva. The plague ceased on the thirty-third day of the Omer (Lag B'Omer) and therefore Jews traditionally observe this day as a minor festival. School may be attended.

Shavuot

This is the Jewish feast to celebrate the giving of the Ten Commandments on Mount Sinai. The festival is also connected with agriculture, and synagogues are usually adorned with flowers and plants. A portion of the Law, including the Ten Commandments, is read in synagogues, and children should not attend school on these two days.

Tish B'av

This is a day of mourning for the destruction of the first and second Temples in Jerusalem.

Rosh Hashanah

On these two days, the New Year, the Jewish people are symbolically judged by God in Heaven, and the Ram's Horn, the Shofar, is blown to awaken the people to repentance.

These two days are among those observed by all Jewish people and children should not attend school. Most Jews, wherever they happen to be, will attend synagogues.

Yom Kippur

This is the Day of Atonement, the tenth day from Rosh Hashanah. It is observed as a fast day from the eve of the day to nightfall on the day itself. During these 25 hours or so, no food or drink touches the lips of Jews and most Jewish people remain in the synagogue throughout the day in worship and contemplation.

Succot or Tabernacles

Succot or Feast of Tabernacles. This is a nine-day (eight days in Israel) festival commemorating the divine protection given to the Israelites during their wanderings through the wilderness. Temporary dwelling places (succot) are erected in the synagogue and meals are taken there. Palm and myrtle branches are waved, symbolic of God's universal presence. Seven circuits of the synagogue are made. The first, second, eighth and ninth are especially holy days, and the eighth involves prayers for rain and recalls the former temple ceremonies of drawing water.

On the first two and the last two days of the festival, Jewish children should not attend school.

Simchath Torah

This the ninth and last day of Succot on which the cycle of the Reading of the Law in synagogues is completed for the year by reading the last section of the Book of Deuteronomy. Another scroll is unwound from which is read the beginning of the Book of Genesis immediately, to demonstrate that the study of the Torah is an everlasting and continuous process.

There is much festivity to celebrate this event, and children play a prominent part in it.

The privilege of reading the last portion of the Law and beginning again is given to members of the synagogue who have been active on behalf of the community.

First Day of Chanucah

This festival commemorates the heroic efforts of the Maccabean brothers to lead the war to oust the Syrian/Greek invaders, who not only ruled Israel at the time but also passed laws proscribing the practice of Judaism, and desecrated the Temple by offering sacrifices in it of unclean animals.

When in 165, before the Common Era, the Syrians were defeated, the Maccabeans made their way to the Temple, cleansed it, reconsecrated it, and re-lit the Menorah, the light of which signified God's presence.

Miraculously, the special oil which was found and which should have lasted for only one day, was found to be enough for eight days, giving the priests enough time to obtain a new consignment of oil.

In commemoration of these events, candles or oil lamps are lit for eight days in Jewish homes.

Jewish children may attend school on these days.

Christianity

Christian disunity

To the Hindu, Muslim or Sikh student embarking on a study of Christianity, a puzzling range of organisations is presented. It is usually something of a mystery that one religion can display such a range of apparently different and independent bodies.

All religions are acquainted with the notion of differences within, and with a spectrum of belief and practice as when, for example, some chose a more strict or ritualistic approach to their religion than others. But in Christianity these differences seem to amount to real divisions, sometimes leading to hostility and conflict.

Desire for unity

Nowadays, many Christians have come to feel that their disunity is something of a scandal and organisations such as the World Council of Churches and the ecumenical movement are manifestations of an attempt on the part of Christians to draw closer together. Occasionally, this movement has resulted in the merging of two separate denominations into one, as in 1972 when the Presbyterian Church in England and the Congregational Church became the United Reformed Church. But the federal approach has been more common, with separate denominations retaining their individual identity and organisation whilst looking for more and more ways to cooperate, including regular meetings for combined worship.

Many Christians will assert that what unites them (belief in Jesus as the Son of God and Saviour of the World, the modelling of their lives on his teaching and example) is infinitely more important than what divides them. Nevertheless, the attachment which Christians display towards their own particular branch of Christianity runs very deep, not least because these separate branches have a long history.

From common origin to great divides

For a thousand years after the death of Jesus, Christians remained united. In the early centuries, through a maze of Councils, Christian doctrine was gradually formalised and ratified, most authoritatively expressed in three creeds known as the Apostles' Creed, the Nicene Creed and the Athanasian Creed.

Eastern and Western Christianity

From the eighth century, however, a breach began to open up between Eastern and Western Christianity in Europe. There were political as well as religious reasons for this, but the most significant doctrinal difference was over one aspect of the Trinity, that fundamental Christian belief that God is Father/Creator, Son and Holy Spirit.

The Eastern branch of the church taught that the Holy Spirit proceeded from the Father alone, whereas the Western branch taught that the Spirit proceeded from the Father *and* the Son. In 1054, this long-standing difference and the East's rejection of the Bishop of Rome's claim of universal jurisdiction and authority over the whole Church, led to the final split between the Roman Catholic or Western Church and the Orthodox or Eastern Church. From that time, the Patriarch of Constantinople has occupied a place of special honour within Orthodox/Eastern Christianity.

There are few Orthodox Christians living in Britain, the best known branches here being the Russian, Greek and Serbian Orthodox Churches.

Continental Reformation

Far more significant for an understanding of the variety of Christian denominations seen in Britain, is the second split which occurred, this time within the Western Church, in the sixteenth century.

41

More and more people were coming to feel a dissatisfaction with the Church, with its power, wealth, conservatism and corruption. On 31 October 1517, a German priest called Martin Luther nailed his 95 theses to a church door in Wittenberg. This document was a detailed attack on what Luther considered to be some of the worst abuses of power on the part of the Church generally, and the Pope (the Bishop of Rome) in particular. There was an immediate sympathetic response to Luther's protest and the University press of Wittenberg could hardly keep pace with the demand (which came from every part of Germany) for copies of the 95 theses.

Luther's protest (hence the name 'Protestant' to describe those who have protested against the authority and certain doctrines of the Roman Catholic Church) was soon echoed in other parts of Europe, most notably in Switzerland where a young Frenchman called John Calvin wrote a classic doctrinal formulation of what now came to be known as the Reformation, 'The Institutes of the Christian Religion'. Basic ideas of the Reformation included an emphasis on the Bible rather than on the Church as authoritative; that people are justified or saved only by faith in Jesus rather than by the good deeds they perform; and that each believer has his or her own direct line to God and does not require the mediation of priest or bishop.

English Reformation

The Reformation ideas were already gaining a hearing in England when, in 1534, King Henry VIII severed connections with Rome and declared that the Church of England was henceforth the 'established Church' with the sovereign as its head. The immediate cause of the breakaway of the English Church was that the Pope had refused to grant Henry an annulment of his marriage to Catherine of Aragon so that he could marry Ann Boleyn. Henry shrewdly tapped the anti-clericalism felt in his kingdom and distributed wealth and property formerly owned by the Church among his nobles, thereby buying their support for his independent English Church. During the reign of his daughter, Elizabeth I, 1558–1603, Protestant Christianity became firmly established in England, though the English Church never departed as radically from the Roman Catholic Church as did other Protestant Churches in Europe. It retained Bishops and Priests (though these were allowed to marry) and a central place was still given to the Holy Communion or Mass.

To this day there are two wings to the Church of England, or Anglican Church, one group emphasising the Catholic aspects of the Church and feeling more in common with Roman Catholics, and another group emphasising Protestant teaching and feeling more at home with other Protestant denominations. 'Catholic' Anglicans, sometimes called 'High Church', favour a more elaborate, ritualistic style of worship, by contrast with the 'Low Church' Anglicans whose worship is similar in form and tone, and closer to other Protestant Churches. Anglicans belong to a particular parish with a rector, vicar or parish priest who is in turn responsible to a bishop who presides over a large geographical area called a diocese. Each diocese has a big mother church called a Cathedral – often a very ancient building with splendid worship and a highly trained choir – where the bishop has his throne (Latin: cathedra = throne).

Doctrinal and organisational differences

Roman Catholics have their parishes, dioceses, and cathedrals organised in a similar way, except that Roman Catholic clergy are not permitted to marry. Other differences include the great reverence and devotion accorded to the Blessed Virgin Mary, the mother of Jesus, and the belief that in the Mass the bread and wine become, in substance, the body and blood of Christ whilst retaining the appearance and taste of bread and wine. In addition, Roman Catholics retain loyalty to the Pope who is regarded as infallible when he speaks on matters of faith or morality.

The logic of division

Thus far it is clear why there are at least two Christian groups in England: Roman Catholics and Anglicans. But what of Baptists, Methodists, Unitarians, Quakers, Open Brethren, the Salvation Army and a number of others? Not surprisingly, once the principle of obedience to the Pope was overthrown by Protestants at the time of the Reformation, and with the emphasis on each believer using his or her own judgement guided by the Scriptures which allow for a variety of interpretations, it was not long before individuals and groups began to set up other Christian organisations or churches where they did not find the Church of England to their liking or where they believed it to be in error.

Baptists

One of the earliest such groups were the Baptists who founded a separate church in England in 1612. Their most characteristic beliefs and practices are clearly implied in their name: they believe that only adults can be baptised since each individual should be old enough to make that decision for himself or herself, and they further believe that baptism must be by total immersion and not by mere sprinkling with water. Baptists do not have bishops and are less hierarchical in their orders of ministry than Roman Catholics or Anglicans.

Methodists

The same is true of Methodists, so called because of the methodical way in which their founders John and Charles Wesley organised study of the Bible and meetings for prayer when they were students at Oxford in the eighteenth century. Later on they travelled the country preaching in the open fields to large congregations and placing great emphasis on the need for each individual believer to undergo a personal experience of conversion, of having their lives or sense of direction dramatically changed. Initially, the Wesley brothers were not intending to set up another Church but to 'revive' the Church of England from within. However, in 1784, the Methodist Church was founded and has become one of the strongest of Protestant Churches in Britain, Australia and the USA.

Quakers

The Society of Friends, or the Quakers, was founded by George Fox in the 1660s. They have no clergy and no set form of service. When they meet in their meeting houses, they wait for God's spirit to guide one of them to speak: sometimes it means that a number of worshippers will stand up to speak but at other times they will sit in complete silence.

Unitarianism

Unitarians affirm the unipersonality of God, as opposed to the doctrine of the Trinity, i.e. three persons in one God. They see Jesus as the great 'humanitarian' exemplar.

As with the Quakers, they have a non-creedal basis for membership. Principles of freedom, reason and tolerance bind the seekers together. In their weekly assemblies there are readings from the Bible from other religions and from secular sources. Major Christian festivals are celebrated with a liberal and modernist interpretation, as are some festivals of other faiths and humanitarian causes.

Although actively and internationally associated with inter-faith movements, Unitarians have recently been excluded from the British Council of Churches.

Salvation Army

The Salvation Army was founded by William Booth in 1865. It is an evangelical movement, respected worldwide for its social work and help to the impoverished. Salvation Army meetings are joyful, led by their famous bands, and often take place on street corners as a witness to their faith. Instead of clergy they organise themselves on military lines with captains, majors, etc. and they do not observe sacraments such as Baptism or Holy Communion.

Pentecostal Churches

The Pentecostal Churches include the Elim Church (1915) and the Assemblies of God (1924). As their names suggest, they place emphasis on the gifts of the Spirit which, it is believed, were first conveyed to Christian believers shortly after the Ascension of Jesus. Most characteristic of these gifts is to be able to speak in an ecstatic, unlearned language other than one's own which can then be interpreted by another worshipper.

Open or Christian Brethren
(sometimes called Plymouth Brethren)

The movement began with a group of Anglicans living in Dublin in 1829. The group members, in wishing to model their lives more closely on the intentions of the original founder, rejected what they later called 'churchianity'.

Although not coordinated by a central administration, the Brethren coalesce into two main bodies namely 'Open' and 'Exclusive' Brethren, descriptions which in part reflect their orientation towards other Christians.

Believing that the second coming is imminent, the Brethren are committed to an urgent evangelism.

Jehovah's Witnesses

Although Jehovah's Witnesses are few in number, they are well known because of their emphasis on home visiting, their strict application of religious principles to certain medical interventions and their frequently-expressed desire to withdraw their children from religious education in schools.

The Church in Scotland, Ireland and Wales

The Established Church in Scotland is the Church of Scotland which is organised on Presbyterian lines. Presbyter is the Greek word for elders. Direction by the elders, senior or respected lay people appears to have been one of the systems of church government in the early Church. Presbyterians lay great emphasis on orderly, dignified worship and strong preaching. Scotland also has the Episcopal Church (Anglican) as well as Roman Catholic and the smaller Protestant Churches. Presbyterianism is also found in Northern Ireland though Roman Catholicism is dominant in the rest of Ireland. The Church in Wales – though Anglican – is separate from the Church of England and dis-established since 1920. The Presbyterian Church is the strongest among other Protestant Churches in Wales.

Celebrations and festivals

It will be clear from this survey of Christian churches that celebrations and festivals are more likely to be observed by those denominations which are most tied to tradition, including the earliest traditions from the time of Jesus and the early Church. Although all Christians celebrate Christmas and Easter, the periods of preparation for these festivals – Advent and Lent – are largely confined in their detailed observance to the Roman Catholic and Anglican churches. These churches adhere closely to a calendar in which all festivals have their appointed time.

Christian Festivals and Holy Days

New Year's Day

C elebrated both as a popular festival and holiday, and by the Church. January 1 is traditionally seen as a time for fresh starts and opportunities. 'A Happy New Year' is a greeting understood by everyone.

The feast of the Circumcision is also on this date, remembering the circumcision of Christ, as is the Jewish custom, eight days after birth.

Epiphany

This festival, twelve days after Christmas, was originally associated with the baptism of Christ, and was one of the main festivals of the early Christians.

In the West it celebrates the manifestation of Christ to the gentiles in the story of the wise men or 'magi'. They brought presents of gold for a king, frankincense for a priest and myrrh for the suffering he would endure. These gifts are presented at the altar in St James's Palace, Chapel Royal by the British royal family. This has been done for the last 700 years.

In Orthodox churches, both on the Vigil (the day before) and on the feast itself, services of Blessing of water take place. The first of these is for the blessing of water in a font or tank for use in church blessings and for the devotional use of the people. The second often takes place outdoors, for the blessing of a local river or spring or even the seaside. The high point of each of these services comes when the priest plunges a cross three times into the water in commemoration of the baptism of Jesus in the Jordan.

In some places where the climate is warm, the priest flings the cross into the sea, and boys are ready to dive to retrieve it.

Week of Prayer for Christian Unity

Special services are held in which members of different denominations visit one another's churches, and pulpits are shared by visiting preachers.

St Brigid's Day

This in Celtic tradition is the first day of spring. Rebirth was associated with Brigantia, the fertility goddess.

In Christian tradition St Brigid (or Bridget), a secondary patron saint of Ireland, is said to have been inspired by the teaching of St Patrick and to have established the first community of nuns in Kildare, an area which is now well known for its racehorses.

Candlemas – Feast of the Purification

This festival celebrates the presentation of Christ in the Temple in Jerusalem 40 days after his birth, as the Jewish custom, and the purification ceremony of the Virgin Mary at the same time.

The English name 'Candlemas' refers to the custom of blessing and distributing candles and carrying them in procession before the mass. The light of the candles is symbolic of Christ as the light of the world.

Shrove Tuesday

Shrove is a term which is associated with confessing sins. The person is said to be shrove or shriven when they have confessed. It is thought necessary to confess sins before the solemnity of Lent which, historically, is a special period of penance for repentant sinners received back into the community or indeed for sinners recognising their frailty who wish to enter the believing and repentant community for the first time.

The day is just before Ash Wednesday which marks the beginning of Lent. The seriousness of Lent was preceded by merrymaking, and people used up all the rich food in the house in preparation for a fast. Pancakes were a good way to use up food, and pancake races are a traditional sport.

The Mardi Gras carnival is now celebrated on an extravagant scale on this day.

The Orthodox equivalent to Shrove Tuesday is Cheese-Fare Week. During the week before Lent begins meat is not eaten. But egg and milk foods, which will not be allowed during Lent itself, are taken. The last day on which meat may be eaten before Easter is the Sunday called Sexagesima in the Western churches.

Ash Wednesday

This marks the first day of Lent. In Roman Catholic churches, the previous year's palm crosses are burnt and the ashes sprinkled with holy water and then an ash cross marked on the participants as a sign of their penance. This is a reminder that sackcloth and ashes were a sign of penance in the Old Testament. Ash Wednesday is a day of fasting in the Catholic Church. As the minister signs each penitent he says,

"Remember man thou art but dust, and into dust you shall return." This reminder of the mortality of man starts the preparation of prayer, penance and meditation for the great Easter festival.

Ash Wednesday commences the great liturgical cycle which culminated in the death and resurrection of Christ on Easter Sunday.

Lent

Ash Wednesday to Holy Saturday – 40 weekdays; Sundays are always festive. This period remembers the 40 days in the wilderness when Christ was tempted. Various degrees of fasting used to be practised but now people usually give up luxuries, give to others and spiritually prepare for Easter.

In the Orthodox (Eastern) Churches, Lent begins two days earlier, on the Monday after the seventh Sunday before Easter. The fasting is strict: not only meat, but eggs and milk products are forbidden. On Sundays, olive oil and wine are allowed, and on Palm Sunday and Annunciation, fish may be eaten as well.

St David's Day

St David is the patron saint of Wales and his feast day has been observed since the fourteenth century. Welsh people wear leeks or daffodils on this day. Very little is known about St David except that he lived in the far south-west of Wales, became an Archbishop and Primate of Wales and advised kings in Ireland.

St Patrick's Day

The patron saint of Ireland is remembered and honoured for his work as a missionary and evangelist. Legend says that as a teenager he was carried off to Ireland from England and later escaped and returned home as a priest to introduce the Christian faith. He built a monastry at Armagh. The Irish celebrate this day as a public holiday and wear the shamrock, which is also a reminder of the Holy Trinity. The deep historic links of Catholicism and nationalism in Ireland are reflected in the St Patrick's Day processions, speech-making, drama and musical activities. In North America, and in the countries where Irish missionaries have been active, celebrations are enthusiastically pursued.

Mothering Sunday

This is held on the fourth Sunday in Lent. It was considered to be a break in the solemnities of Lent, being a cheerful day when girls in service visited their mothers, taking simnel cakes as presents. These cakes were generally kept until Easter. People in villages also went to the Mother Church to give gifts. Today it is celebrated by people buying cards and flowers for their mother and giving her a day of rest. Churches often provide flowers and cards for children to give to their mothers.

Palm Sunday

This marks the beginning of Holy Week, the last week of Jesus's life on earth, and celebrates the story of Jesus entering Jerusalem on a donkey, when he was welcomed by crowds waving palm branches (Matthew 21, 1-9).

Processions are made around churches and between churches, carrying and distributing branches or fronds of palms. Churches are usually decorated with palms or willow. Crosses shaped from palms are often distributed to the congregation on Palm Sunday.

Maundy Thursday

This day begins a special commemoration of the last acts of Jesus's life and remembers the Last Supper which Jesus shared with his disciples where he gave the commandment to 'Love one another', washed their feet and instituted the Eucharist. (Maundy comes from the Latin word 'mandatum' meaning command.)

In England, the monarch or his/her representative washed and kissed the feet of the poor and gave them money up until the time of Queen Anne. The Georges discontinued the washing – or rather commuted it to a further gift of coin. The Royal Almoner still wears a folded towel at the Maundy ceremony, in case the monarch were to revive the custom!

Good Friday

This Friday before Easter Day is the day on which the anniversary of the crucifixion of Christ is kept. It is a day of fast, abstinence and penance in some churches, but in others – notably the Free Churches – it has become a feast day.

It is called Good Friday because Christians believe that because Jesus died for mankind, everything will be right between them and God. His love and his sacrifice are remembered.

Services are usually held in churches, sometime between noon and 3.00 p.m. when as Mark (15, 33–34) says, Jesus died on the cross. There are often united services and processions and passion plays portraying the Easter events.

Hot cross buns are eaten. They used to be kept specially for Good Friday with the symbolism of the cross, although it is thought that they originated in pagan times with the bun representing the moon and its four quarters.

Holy Saturday

This the last day of Holy Week, once known as the 'Great Sabbath' and now also known as Easter Eve. It commemorates the period during which Jesus lay in the tomb after he had been taken down from the cross.

The day is traditionally honoured as a focus upon the forgiveness of sins.

Easter Sunday

This is the most important festival in the Christian Church, celebrating the resurrection of Jesus. Traditionally it is the day when new members are baptised into the Christian community and comes at the end of Lent, which is a period of preparation for the great event.

Easter is often celebrated with a midnight mass where the priest lights one large candle from which the many smaller candles of the congregation take light and pass on the flame, while the people say or sing "Christ is risen". Dawn services and outdoor services are quite common on Easter Day.

The word 'Easter' is connected with the Anglo-Saxon spring goddess Eostre, and it seems that Christian celebrations displaced the pagan festival. The custom of giving eggs is an ancient one celebrating new life. People often spring-clean or decorate and make a fresh start at Easter. New clothes are worn and there are Easter parades.

The date of Easter is determined by the paschal full moon and can be anywhere between 21 March and 25 April. There was early controversy whether Easter should follow the fixed lunar month and be celebrated at the time of the Jewish Passover, and various churches celebrated it at different times. The Alexandrian calculation was accepted in the year 325, but in the fourth and fifth centuries the Roman Church disagreed. In Britain, the Celtic churches had their own system of calculations, but the Roman method was adopted by the Synod of Whitby in the year 664.

St George's Day

St George became patron saint of England during the reign of Edward III, when the Order of the Garter was founded under the saint's patronage. Although once a very prominent holy day in the Christian calendar, St George's Day is today celebrated mainly by special parades and rallies. Many legends have been built up around the figure of St George, but all that is known with a degree of certainty is that he suffered martyrdom in Palestine, before the reign of the Roman Emperor Constantine, where he may have been a soldier in the Roman Army.

Ascension Day

This is kept on the Thursday which is the fortieth day after Easter. It commemorates Christ's last earthly appearance to his disciples after the resurrection and his ascension into heaven into divine glory, which traditionally happened on the Mount of Olives (See Mark 16, 19, Luke 24–51 and Acts 1, 1–11.)

The purpose of the commemoration is to remember that Christ's spirit lives on. In the Western Church, the paschal candle lit during Easter is extinguished on Ascension Day in commemoration of Christ's departure from the apostles.

Christian Aid Week

This is a week in which Christians focus on the need to care both spiritually and materially for people everywhere. Third World countries are especially remembered both in special prayers and the raising of funds. The organisation of 'Christian Aid' usually has a theme for raising money, such as the provision of wells for villages.

Whit Sunday or Pentecost

This is held on the fiftieth day after Easter and commemorates the gift of the Holy Spirit to the followers of Christ. It is often called Pentecost because when the disciples received the Holy Spirit and began to go out and preach about Jesus it was the Jewish festival of Pentecost.

Because it marked the first preaching about Jesus, it is called the birthday of the Christian Church. It is a favourite day for baptism. As converts are often dressed in white for baptism it was probably originally 'White Sunday'. It is marked by miracle or mystery plays and processions, particularly in the north of England where the 'Whit Walk' is common and new clothes are worn. It is a major Christian festival and celebrated as a Holy Day of Obligation in the Catholic Church.

Corpus Christi

Corpus Christi, literally the Body of Christ, is celebrated on the Thursday after Whit week. In the Catholic Church it is a Holy Day of Obligation in which people are expected to attend church.

It celebrates the institution of the Eucharist at the Last Supper. The Eucharist is celebrated on the Thursday of Holy Week but, being placed then between the austerity of Ash Wednesday and the dramatic tragedy of Good Friday, a joyous commemoration is difficult.

Feast of St Peter and St Paul

Saints Peter and Paul are seen as two powerful pillars of the Christian Church. Peter became the first Bishop of Rome, and Paul took the Christian message with vigour and eloquence to a new gentile audience.

This is a Holy Day of Obligation in the Catholic Church.

In the Orthodox Church this feast is preceded by a fast, which begins on the Monday eight days after Whit Sunday. The earlier Easter comes, the longer the Sts Peter and Paul fast!

Assumption of the Blessed Virgin

This feast is celebrated in the Roman Catholic and Orthodox Churches to commemorate the resurrection of the Virgin Mary, believed taken body and soul into heaven immediately after death. The Feast of the Assumption dates from the sixth century and in many Western European countries the day is observed both for its religious significance and as a public holiday.

In the Orthodox Church this festival is observed as the Falling Asleep of the Blessed Virgin Mary. Pope Pius XII declared the Corporal Assumption of the Blessed Virgin as an official dogma of the Catholic Church. Protestants reject this doctrine.

Harvest Festival

This is one of the oldest festivals known to man. After prayers for a good harvest, it seemed natural to give offerings or sacrifice part of the crops. The Jews celebrate three harvest festivals dating from their wanderings in the wilderness with Moses. In Christian Britain, harvest is an unofficial religious festival of thanksgiving, usually observed on a Sunday in September or October to give thanks for the harvest being gathered in.

Since the middle of the last century, the custom of displaying fruits, vegetables and flowers in the Church of England and the Free Churches has developed, and these are later given to charitable causes.

In medieval times, Lammas Day, August 1, was a celebration of the offering of the first fruits (Deut 26, 1–11). A loaf made from the first grain was baked and used in the Eucharist. The service was called Loaf Mass, in Saxon 'Half Masse', which gradually became Lammas. The arrival of Lammas Day also meant that the Lammas Land in some villages could be used for general grazing of stock by all villagers as the hay would have already been reaped. Country fairs were also held around Lammas Day.

When all the harvest had been gathered in, Harvest Home would be celebrated at the farmer's house, with a supper. The last of the corn would be twisted into a person or cross corn dolly. It was believed that the corn spirit was contained in the dolly and had to be kept alive during the winter and sown with the new corn to ensure a good harvest. It was often taken to the church for the harvest service before being hung in the barn. Some churches still have harvest suppers.

In seaside towns, churches may celebrate a harvest of the sea, and in some manufacturing towns, tools or machinery may now replace the traditional displays. Special hymns are sung and the Church of England has a special service.

Advent

The four Sundays preceding Christmas Day, 25 December, are called the four Sundays of Advent.

Advent is the season when the Christian celebrates his condition between the two comings, the coming of Christ on the first Christmas and the second and final coming of Christ to deliver the world from darkness.

The scriptural readings during this season manifest a Christian sense of history together with a joyful expectancy. John the Baptist, the precursor of Jesus, is given a prominence as are the thoughts of certainty, preparedness and joy in the future. Matthew 3, 1–12 'John the Baptist appeared; he preached in the wilderness of Judea and this was his message, "Repent, for the kingdom of heaven is close at hand."' Romans 13, 11–14 'Wake up, our salvation is even nearer now than it was when we were converted.'

All Saints' Day (All Hall)

This festival celebrates Christian saints known and unknown. Although it was originally held in May, its date is now November 1 and probably stems from Gregory III (died 741) who dedicated a chapel to 'All Saints' at St Peter's Basilica on that day, and Gregory IV (died 844) ordered its universal observation. In the Eastern Church it is still kept on the first Sunday after Whitsun. It is a Roman Catholic Holy Day of Obligation; Roman Catholics are expected to attend church.

All Souls' Day

This festival has been kept for nearly one thousand years. A shipwrecked pilgrim was told by a hermit that the souls of the dead who had not yet gone to heaven were crying out because people were not praying enough for them. The pilgrim told Odila, Abbot of Cluny, who set aside the day after All Saints' Day as All Souls' Day. Christians pray for the souls of the dead and often take flowers to the family grave.

As the Orthodox Churches do not observe All Saints' in November, neither do they observe this All Souls' Day. But they have several similar days in their calendar, on which the dead are especially prayed for: most notably the Saturday before Lent and the Tuesday after Low Sunday.

St Andrew's Day

St Andrew is the patron saint of Scotland, of Greece, and of Russia. Andrew was a disciple of Jesus and the brother of Peter. Not much is known about him, except that traditionally he was crucified on an X-shaped cross and that in the thirteenth century some monks brought his relics to Scotland to secure their own protection.

In the Anglican Church the day is used to make intercessions for foreign missions.

Feast of the Immaculate Conception

Popular early Christian devotion to the Virgin Mary was confirmed at the Council of Ephesus in 431 when she was proclaimed to be the Mother of God. In subsequent centuries Christians, both Eastern and Western, advanced and extended devotion to the Virgin Mary. In honour of her special position in the history of mankind's redemption, the redemptive effects of her life, death and resurrection of Jesus were anticipated at her birth. In 1854, Pope Pius IX declared that Mary as the Immaculate Conception was conceived free from original sin.

Four years after the declaration of Pius IX, a young French girl, Bernadette Soubirous, had a vision of Mary at Lourdes. In the apparition Mary introduced herself as the 'Immaculate Conception'. Since then Catholics from all over the world have flocked to Lourdes in pilgrimage. Pilgrims find that the great chorus of hymns, the torchlight processions and the rows of hopeful sick create a deep sense of pilgrimage.

The Orthodox Churches observe a feast on the Conception of the Theotokos, but they reject the papal doctrine of the immaculate conception because they say it is based on a faulty quasi-Calvinistic doctrine of original sin.

Christmas Eve

On Christmas Eve carol services and midnight masses are held at churches and cathedrals throughout the world to celebrate the birth of Christ.

Christmas Day

This festival celebrates the birth of Christ. Although it is likely that Jesus was born at a different time of the year, December 25 was used, probably to coincide with and to change the Roman festival of the birthday of the unconquered sun. (December 21/22 is now the shortest day of the year due to a calendar correction in 1752.)

The first Christians did not keep Christmas, but by the fourth century, it was celebrated. January 6, which was used a lot in the East, was originally used for a commemoration of a heresy that 'divine Christ appeared' only at his baptism by John. The Eastern Church still uses Epiphany (or appearing) whereas the Western Church adopted December 25 because Rome did so between 336 and 353.

Although our calendar dates from Christ's birth, there have been miscalculations. Jesus was born when Herod was king and the Romans were ruling, and Herod died in what we refer to as 4 BC. The Roman calendar was used when Jesus was born and continued to be used until the sixth century. In AD 533, a Russian monk named Dionysius made the Christian calendar but miscalculated. It is reckoned Jesus was born sometime between 7 BC and 4 BC.

Christmas is celebrated with joy and merry-making. Friends and families get together and give presents, remembering the gift of Christ and the gifts given to Jesus. Peace and goodwill to all men is proclaimed in the singing of Christmas carols. Often candlelight services are held.

It was a belief of the church fathers that Christ, in the perfection of his life, lived a perfect (complete) number of years. Therefore, the date of his death ought to be the date of his conception. Early astronomers reckoned that Good Friday AD 34 was

25 March. Therefore, the feast of the Annunciation of the Angel to Mary was 25 March, and the Nativity of Christ, December 25. The suggestion that Christmas was deliberately invented to replace Sol Invicta, was first mooted by the Puritans, who hated the joy of Christmas, and revived by the Deists and their successors, who hated the religion of Christmas.

Christmas Customs

Many of the modern Christmas customs are directly derived from ceremonies associated with ancient mid-winter feasts. One of the oldest is probably the decoration of houses and churches with greenery. Evergreens – the symbol of everlasting life – were commonly used to decorate dwellings and sacred buildings in ancient times at the time of the winter solstice, and the custom has endured despite the efforts of the early Christian Church to put an end to the practice.

Holly and ivy were the favourite plants, although laurel was also used. Mistletoe, sacred to the Druids, was used in houses but it was, and still is, banned from some churches. The custom of kissing under the mistletoe is entirely English in origin.

The Christmas tree is a relative newcomer to England. It came originally from Germany, and went to America with the German settlers before it reached the British Isles sometime in the early nineteenth century. The first English Christmas tree of which there is any clear record was one set up at a children's party by a member of Queen Caroline's Court in 1821. The custom of having a Christmas tree as an important symbol of the festival, however, became widespread only after Prince Albert, the Consort of Queen Victoria, set up one at Windsor Castle in 1841.

Since 1947, the Norwegian capital, Oslo, has made an annual gift of an immense Christmas tree to the people of London. This stands brightly lit, in Trafalgar Square, close to Nelson's Monument.

Many churches now have a Christmas crib, although not so long ago these were rarely seen except in Roman Catholic churches and homes. Tradition says it was St Francis of Assisi who made the first crib in 1224.

Exchanging presents and Christmas cards are essential features of the Christmas festival, though the custom has its roots in pre-Christian times. Presents were given to the poor and relatives at the feast of the Saturnalia in ancient Rome. The Christmas card began its existence as the 'Christmas piece' – a decorated sheet of paper on which school children wrote polite greetings for the season in their best handwriting and presented these to their parents.

Father Christmas is the traditional bearer of gifts in Britain. Originally he was more the personification of the joys of Christmas than a gift-giver. He is mentioned in a fifteenth-century carol which began, 'Hail, Father Christmas, hail to thee!' and has been a familiar figure for centuries. Parliament abolished him in 1644 but he came back after the Restoration. In the nineteenth century he acquired some of the attributes of the Teutonic Santa Klaus and now children think of him as the bearer of gifts, coming at night from the North Pole in his reindeer-drawn sleigh and entering homes through the chimneys.

The Yule log was one of the main features of Christmas festivities in England and other European countries. The traditional log was usually of oak or ash and as large as the widest fireplace in the house would allow. It was brought in on Christmas Eve with great ceremony and rejoicing and lit with a fragment of its predecessor of the year before. It had to burn steadily throughout the twelve days of Christmas and at the end was put out, and a portion saved to use in kindling the next year's log so that there would be a continuity of good fortune and blessing. It was never allowed to burn away completely.

Christmas food has been largely a matter of tradition. Turkey, the most usual dish on Christmas day, did not appear in Britain until about 1542 and was not very popular until much later. Its predecessors were goose and pork, or a huge Christmas pie made from a variety of birds. In richer houses, venison, swans or peacocks were eaten. However, the boar's head was always considered to be the most succulent dish of all. It was usually brought to the table on a gold or silver platter and with great ceremony.

The ancestor of the modern Christmas pudding was plum porridge – a mixture of meat broth, raisins, spices, fruit and wine. When puddings are made at home, every member of the family is expected to make a wish while waiting their turn to stir it. A few small charms such as a silver coin (promising wealth), a ring (promising speedy marriage) and a thimble (prophesying a single life) are included in the mixture.

The tradition of eating mince pies is older than plum pudding as they were already well known by the end of the sixteenth century. They were originally more varied in content, including items such as chopped chicken, eggs, spices and raisins, all contained in little pastry cases known as 'coffins'. According to tradition, one should be eaten on each of the twelve days of Christmas to ensure twelve happy months in the coming year.

In England, the traditional Christmas drink was the wassail which was always served in a large brown vessel made of apple wood. It consisted of ale, roast apples, eggs, sugar, nutmegs, cloves and ginger and was drunk while hot.

Wassail comes from two old Saxon words, 'was haile' meaning 'your health'. In Victorian times, the wassail bowl was carried from door to door in rural areas. Neighbours would fill the bowl with ale or cider to ensure a good apple harvest the next autumn.

Carols were never considered to be religious hymns. Rather, they were the popular songs of the Christian religion which came into being after the religious revival of the thirteenth century. Puritanism swept away the English carols and they did not come back into general favour for nearly 200 years. Now, nearly all churches have a carol service and groups of children go from home to home, singing carols and being rewarded with mince pies and money.

December 26 is the feast of St Stephen, the first Christian martyr. In England, this anniversary is popularly known as Boxing Day. The name is thought to be derived later from the alms boxes in churches which were opened on this day and their contents distributed among the poor, or else from the earthenware boxes apprentices carried when they were collecting gifts of money from their master's customers. Until recently it was usual for the postman, dustman and other public employees to call at the houses they served to receive small gifts.

For over 800 years, one of the regular Christmas entertainments was mumming, when young men and women dressed up, sometimes in each others clothes, wore masks and gave a display of dancing or enacted a play at the homes of the rich people. They were usually rewarded with a gift of money or food.

In the course of time, the dialogue and action underwent several changes, although the central theme continued to be the victory of good over evil. At the end of the play, there was usually some clowning and gaiety in which all the characters would join.

Plays about the nativity were part of miracle plays, which became popular between the thirteenth century and sixteenth century. They were based on Bible stories and were originally performed as part of a church service.

The Reformation checked the popularity of miracle plays and gave rise to the morality play, which was mainly concerned with the behaviour of men and women.

Pantomime is an entirely British form of

entertainment. It is believed to have originated in the eighteenth century and continues to be a popular feature of Christmas festivities and celebrations.

Orthodox Christian Christmas Customs

Christmas in the Orthodox Christian tradition is marked by various distinctive customs. To symbolise Christ's entry into the world, a young oak tree is brought home, placed on the fire and burned on Christmas Eve. At the same time, straw is spread on the floor. A prayer service is conducted, after which a festive supper is served.

The first visitor to the home on Christmas morning has special significance in many East European countries. He/she represents the shepherds who had the honour to see and announce the birth of Christ.

Chesnica, a simple bread and nut pastry, is prepared on Christmas Day, with a silver or gold coin baked into it. It is cut open during the Christmas meal and the person served the piece with the coin is supposed to have good luck in the coming year.

Christmas customs are crowned with going to church for the Divine Liturgy.

Sikhism

The later half of the fifteenth century witnessed the emergence of a vigorous new religious movement in the Indian subcontinent. The doctrines and beliefs essential to this faith found expression in a distinctive way of life, which its practitioners refer to as the **'Gurmat'** (the Guru's doctrine) but is known more generally as Sikhism.

The fundamental principles of Sikhism were laid down by its founder, Guru Nanak, and by the continuous line of Gurus who succeeded him.

Essentially monotheistic, God in the Sikh scriptures is described as formless, eternal and immanent in all creation. Consequently, living in this world is not a bondage (for the soul) but a rare opportunity to attain God. Salvation or deliverance from accumulated sins can be obtained through good deeds as well as by the grace of God.

Guru Nanak, who was a practical man with a love for God's creation as well as for God in himself, preached truthful living under the three headings **Naam** (remembering God), **Kirat** (working hard) and **Wand** (sharing food).

Grace is obtained by the repetition of God's name. Guru Nanak explaining God's grace in us said: "Mind is the paper on which are recorded our deeds, good or bad, as the sum of our cumulative actions dictates. But the Almighty is merciful for he can turn dross into gold and extinguish all passions and wanderings and obliterate all accumulated sins."

The concept of the Guru is central to Sikh belief and practice. Sikhism does not advocate asceticism and withdrawal from the world as a way of achieving salvation. On the other hand, service to society is encouraged. Great importance is also attached to congregational worship as a means of acquiring Enlightenment.

The history of Sikhism can be largely understood as the gradual institutionalisation of a religious truth as revealed to its founder Guru Nanak and preached by his successors. The tenth guru, Guru Gobind Singh, formalised the identification of Sikhs into the **Khalsa Panth** – organisation of Saint Soldier. The Khalsa endeavours to create a union of all those who love God and serve humanity, and respects the adherents of all other faiths irrespective of the differences of creed and ways of worship. Members of the Khalsa are distinguished by five external symbols, often called the five 'K's. These are: Kesh (uncut hair), Kanda (a comb), Kirpan (sword), Karaha (steel bracelet worn on the right wrist), Kacha (knee-length shorts).

Sikh Festivals

The birth and death anniversaries of Guru Nanak and the nine Gurus who succeeded him are important events in the Sikh calendar and are marked by both religious and secular celebrations. The spring festival of Baisakhi commemorates the creation of the Khalsa. In recent years the superb religious celebration of the festival in the Golden Temple, Amritsar, has been broadcast live by Sunrise Radio, the Asian radio station which broadcasts throughout the south-east of England on 1458 KHz and across Europe on satellite.

After the assassination of Guru Gobind Singh in 1708, the line of human Gurus came to an end and the spiritual leadership of the Sikh community came to be vested in the holy scriptures – the **Guru Granth Sahib.** Sikh worship takes place in its presence and on important occasions the Guru Granth Sahib is read from beginning to end without a break.

Lohri

Lohri is the winter festival of Punjab and is celebrated by Hindus and Sikhs. The night of Lohri is considered to be the coldest night of the year and the festivities usually take place around bonfires. For many days before this festival, children go around people's houses singing folk songs, in return for which they are given either money or special items of food.

Lohri has particular significance in families with a newborn baby or a newly-married son. Dried fruits, nuts, sesame snaps, popcorn and rice flakes are eaten and also distributed to relatives, friends and neighbours. It is customary to throw rice flakes, sesame seeds and popcorn into the bonfire for luck. A young bride is encouraged to throw black sesame seeds (which are rare), into the fire because it is believed she will have as many sons as the seeds she throws.

On the next day, which marks the beginning of the month of Magha or Maghi, Sikhs go to the Gurdwara (Sikh place of worship) to join in the celebrations commemorating the new month. The town of Muktsar in the Punjab is the scene of a big fair held every year in memory of the tenth Guru Gobind Singh and forty Sikh martyrs.

Basant Panchami

This is the festival heralding the arrival of spring. It falls on the fifth day after Magh in the Vikram calendar. Fields turn yellow with mustard flowers and people dress themselves in yellow clothes. The Namdhari Sikhs celebrate this day as the birthday of their founder, Guru Ram Singh Ji.

Holla Mohalla

In 1680 at Anandpur, India, Guru Gobind Singh, the tenth guru of the Sikhs, introduced the festival of Holla Mohalla as an alternative to the Hindu festival of Holi. There are displays of swordsmanship, horsemanship, archery, wrestling competitions, display of weapons and poetic symposia, making it a very colourful festival in the Sikh calendar.

Baisakhi/Vaisakhi

Baisakhi is the north Indian harvest festival celebrated in the spring season. At that time wheat, the staple crop of the area, is ready for harvest and the farmer celebrates the fruit of his hard work with celebrations involving songs and bhangra dance (harvest-folk dance). It is also New Year's Day in the State of the Punjab and it usually falls on 13 April (occasionally on 14 April as in 1999 and 2002).

The founder of the Sikh faith, Guru Nanak Dev, started his missionary travels on this day, and so the third guru, Guru Amar Das, asked his disciples to gather on this day and celebrate it as a special festival, distinct from other faiths, to give the Sikhs a separate and individual identity. It continued in much the same way until the time of Guru Gobind Singh, the tenth guru who, in 1699, chose the festival as the birthday of the Sikh nation.

Guru Gobind Singh had earlier commanded his followers, spread across various parts of India, to gather together on Baisakhi Day 1699. They came from far and wide and on the actual day, over a hundred thousand had assembled for the morning prayer at Anandpur (literally 'the town of bliss'). This had been founded by Guru Gobind Singh's father, the ninth guru, Guru Teg Bahadur.

After the early morning prayers, the Guru addressed the congregation, then drew out his sword in a flash and demanded the head of a Sikh who would be willing to die for (dharam) his faith. This was a strange demand coming from a guru who had won the hearts of his followers by helping the needy, the oppressed and the down-trodden. In setting up a democratic mechanism for leading mankind, Guru Gobind Rai wanted to select five people who were liberated from the bondage of the physical body.

Some people panicked and left the congregation, others stayed, but the silence was such that one could hear a pin drop. Then one man, Daya Ram, offered his head to the Guru. He was taken inside a tent/marquee which was erected near the platform from where the Guru was addressing the huge gathering. The congregation heard the strike of the sword. The next moment the Guru was back before the congregation with the same sword dripping with blood and demanded another head. There was consternation in the audience, yet another man mustered courage and offered his head to the Guru. It happened five times in all. Then the Guru brought all five men back to the congregation adorned in identical attire and, it is said, there was a certain aura around them.

Another remarkable fact was that the men's names symbolised kindness, righteousness, courage, steadfastness and leadership – values which all Sikhs are encouraged to believe in and to uphold.

Guru Gobind Singh then baptised the five chosen men with a special nectar called Amrit which he prepared in an iron bowl and to which his wife (Mata Sahib Kaur) added sugar crystals. The Guru recited Gurbani (holy scriptures) throughout this process, whilst stirring the mixture with the Kirpan (the double-edged sword). Subsequently the Guru asked the already baptised Sikhs to now baptise him. Thus the brotherhood of the Sikhs was born, known as the Khalsa – a democratic arrangement in which the Guru and his Sikh followers became equal participants.

After the initiation ceremony, the Guru asked them to follow a code of conduct (the Sikh 'Rahit Maryada'), which consisted of having the second name 'Singh' (which means lion) for men and 'Kaur' (meaning princess) for women. Gender and social equality was enshrined in the very formalisation of Sikhism. The five symbols, all commencing with the letter 'K' in the original Punjabi, were given at the same time.

For the Sikhs, Baisakhi is an important festival, but the Baisakhi of 1919 is especially remembered as the Jallianwala Bagh massacre. Then General Dyer, the Commissioner of Amritsar, considering it to be a political meeting, fired on a large crowd of people including many children who had congregated in the walled park to celebrate this historic day. Nowadays it is celebrated amongst the Punjabis all over the world as a religious, social and political occasion.

For some years now, the Sikh community in England has contributed funds to the Golden Temple Broadcasting Appeal, to make it possible for Sunrise Radio to broadcast live from Amritsar during the three days of celebration there. Each year the Celebrations become more and more popular here.

Guru Arjan Dev's Martyrdom Day

Guru Arjan Dev, the fifth guru of the Sikhs, was the first Sikh martyr. By the time of his leadership, the Sikh faith had developed into a well organised and established religion, with missionary centres in all the major towns and districts in what was then the north-west of India, particularly in the State of Punjab. Towns such as Kartarpur, Goindwal and Amritsar, which had been established by the previous Gurus, enjoyed trading activities and flourishing skills. Women and lower castes were treated equally with higher castes. A strong Sikh community was taking shape.

Guru Arjan Dev was a man of the masses and wielded great influence. His growing power and prestige roused the jealousy of the Emperor Jahangir. It is said that a plot was hatched, as a result of which Guru Arjan Dev was suspected of supporting the dissident Prince Khusrau against the Mughal Emperor Jahangir. Guru Arjan Dev was asked to:

1. Change the text of Guru Granth Sahib.
2. Pay a fine of 2 000 000 Rupees.

Guru Arjan Dev refused to pay the fine or to change the Guru Granth Sahib. The Guru was incarcerated at Lahore in the custody of Chandal Lal, a Hindu minister at Lahore Court and was sentenced to be tortured to death. Guru Arjan was starved for three days. On the fourth day he was taken out and forced to sit on a red-hot iron plate. Then burning hot sand was poured over the Guru's body. Burnt and blistered, the Guru was taken to the River Ravi under a strong escort. The Guru plunged into the water and was never seen again.

Guru Arjan Dev is celebrated in Sikh history as an apostle of peace and learning and the day of his martyrdom is celebrated as the victory of good over evil.

The First Presentation of Adi Granth

Adi Granth was presented to the Sikh congregation for the first time by the fifth Guru, Arjan Dev, in 1604. Before that, Gurbani (word of God revealed through Sikh Gurus) of the first four gurus was written in four different parts. Guru Arjan Dev collected together, not only the Gurbani or poetical divine utterances of the earlier gurus, but also the poetry of both Hindu and Muslim saints (including so-called low caste and untouchables) who believed in one God and the equality of all humans – thus making it as the 'Bible of the universal religion'. The total collection comprises 6204 shabads (hymns) compiled in 31 different ragas (musical modes).

The first presentation of the Adi Granth was made in Harmandir Sahib which was built by the fifth Guru in the town of Amritsar. Hari means God, while Mandir means house. Hence Harmandir is the House of God. There is an interesting universality about the Harmander Sahib itself. The foundation stone was laid by a Muslim divine, Saint Main Mir. It has four entrances in four directions offering a welcome to all irrespective of caste, colour, creed, country or sex.

The first granthi (priest, specialist in sacred text) appointed by Guru Arjan Dev was Baba Budha Jee.

Guru Ram Das

Guru Ram Das was born on 24 September 1534 in Chuna Mandi, Lahore. Being the first son of the family, he was called Jetha. His father, Hari Das, who belonged to the Sodhi caste, was a petty trader, and even as a child Jetha had to supplement his income by selling boiled grams (black chick peas).

He lost his mother at an early age, and when he was seven lost his father too. His maternal grandmother took him away to live with her, where he had to spend his days in poverty. When he was twelve, his grandmother decided to leave her village and move to Goindwal, a city founded by Guru Amar Das (the third guru) on the banks of the River Beas, and they settled there.

At Goindwal, Ram Das began to live a life dedicated to the Guru's cause and would do any job for the Guru. He was privileged to meet Guru Angad Dev, the second Guru. He learnt the science of music and acquired mastery over the art of poetry and mythology and of the sacred compositions of the Gurus.

In 1552, Guru Angad Dev passed on his guruship (apostolate) to Amar Das and in 1553, struck by the manifold qualities of Ram Das, Guru Amar Das decided to give to him the hand of his daughter, Bibi Bhani, in marriage. Ram Das stayed with his father-in-law and was closely associated with his ministry.

He commanded the full confidence of the Guru, and for this reason he deputised for the Guru in the court of King Akbar and accompanied him on a long journey to Hardwar to acquaint the people with his religion. Guru Amar Das was so impressed by him that in 1574 he got down from his seat, seated Ram Das there, and placed five paisas and one coconut before him as a mark of handing over to him the Gurgadhi.

Soon after the marriage of his daughter to Ram Das, Guru Amar Das had asked him to start a new settlement on wasteland near the village of Sultanwind, which was then named as Guru Ka Chak. A low-lying area with a small pond in the east of this settlement was also excavated into a bigger pool. Later, both the settlement and the pool were further developed by Guru Arjan who renamed them as 'Ramdas Pur' and 'Amritsar' (Amrit means nectar and sar means pool). Thus, the settlement around this pool of nectar, which developed into a thriving town, became known as Amritsar.

Guru Ram Das also composed the Sikh wedding hymns, which form a very important part of the Sikh marriage ceremony.

Sikh Diwali

The Sikhs celebrate Diwali in honour of the sixth guru, Guru Hargobind. He was the son of Guru Arjan, the fifth Guru. Guru Hargobind became the sixth guru after his father was assassinated by the Mughals for refusing to change his faith in 1606.

Guru Hargobind was only eleven at that time. He decided to defend himself and his people by wearing the two swords of 'miri' and 'piri' – symbols of political and religious leadership. He also refused to pay the fine imposed on his father for preaching his religion.

On these grounds the officers of the Mughal Emperor Jehangir imprisoned him at the fort of Gwalior where he stayed in prison for about five years. Eventually, Jehangir examined the case personally and ordered the Guru's release.

Sharing his prison were 52 Hindu princes, who were not offered their liberty. Guru Hargobind said that he would only accept his release if the princes were also allowed to leave the prison with him. The reply of the prison officers was that as many princes as could pass through the narrow passage of the prison, holding on to the Guru's clothes, could go free.

The Guru ordered a cloak to be made which had long tassel-like ends. All the princes walked to freedom holding on to his train. That is why the Sikhs call Guru Hargobind 'Bandi-Chor' – the releaser of prisoners.

When the Guru returned to Amritsar in 1620, the Sikhs illuminated the Golden Temple in honour of his release. Thus Diwali has a special meaning. It symbolises freedom of conscience, freedom to practise one's own faith, to respect another person's faith and to fight persecution. Later, his grandson, Guru Gobind Singh, said, "There is only one race – the human race." Everybody is invited to share in the celebrations.

On Diwali day, Sikhs from far and wide gather in the precincts of the Golden Temple from early morning. At night the temple and the surrounding buildings are illuminated with candles, lamps and electric bulbs.

The reflections of illuminations in the pool surrounding the Golden Temple add to the beauty and grandeur of the temple. There are also firework displays. Treasures accumulated during the Sikh rule are put on show and a general gala atmosphere pervades the town. In Britain, too, people decorate their homes and use candles and coloured light bulbs to illuminate them. Sweets and presents are exchanged. People go to worship at the Gurdwaras and other holy places, which are specially decorated for the occasion.

Succession of Guru Granth Sahib

It is said that three days before his passing away, Guru Gobind Singh ended the human succession to Guruship and installed the 'Adi Granth' as Sri Guru Granth Sahib in 1708. The word Guru means a guide or a teacher, a dispeller of the darkness of ignorance by sharing the light of spiritual knowledge with the world. The 1430-page Holy Book contains writings of the Gurus and Hindu and Muslim saints, thereby making it a universal book of prayer. It occupies the central place in a Sikh Gurdwara.

Guru Nanak's Birthday

Guru Nanak was born in the fifteenth century in the plains of the Punjab. He was born on 20 October, 1469 (15 April according to some scholars) in Rai Bhoe ki Talwandi, now known as Nankana Sahib in the Sheikupur district of West Pakistan. His father, Mehta Kalu, was a patwari, fairly high in the revenue department. His mother's name was Tripta and he had an elder sister named Nanki, four years his senior.

Guru Nanak was the founder of the Sikh religion and the first guru of the Sikhs. He was followed by nine successive gurus.

When he was five years old, like many other children he was sent to an elementary school. He also attended Brij Nath's school for two years and was introduced to the Vedas (ancient scriptures) and philosophy. He was then sent to a Muslim teacher to learn Persian and Arabic to get a good post in a department of the government. He made himself familiar with the popular creeds both of the Muslims and the Hindus and he gained a general knowledge of the Quran and the brahmanical shastras. He displayed a remarkable grasp of the Vedic Upanishadic (philosophical dispositions), Quranic, Arabic and other philosophical literature.

At nine, he was required by custom to invest himself with the sacred thread 'Janaeu', as the Hindus call it, but he refused to do so, saying that he would rather have a thread that would neither break nor get soiled nor be burnt or lost. (The ceremony of investing with the sacred thread is, strictly speaking, a Brahmin custom of confirmation in which a cotton cord is placed on an 8 to 10-year-old male. It is worn over the shoulder and across the chest. The twisted cotton thread is slightly thinner than a pencil.) The Guru's view of the custom was:

'Out of the cotton of compassion spin the thread of contentment. Tie ends of continence, give it the twist of truth. Make such a sacred thread for the mind. Such a thread once worn will never break nor get soiled, burnt or lost. The man who weareth such a thread is blessed.'

His mind was so fixed on God that he would constantly sing his praise and meditate on his name. To take him out of this mood, his father tried him in various professions. He was sent to a neighbouring town with 20 Rupees to buy goods of common use and sell them at a profit. On the way he came across a group of faqirs (saints) who had been hungry for several days. Guru Nanak spent his money feeding them. He felt that he had struck a real bargain in doing so as he understood that it was more profitable to feed mankind in need than to make purely monetary profit. His father did not understand the Guru's reasoning and flew into a rage and slapped his son.

At the age of sixteen he married, then had two sons. In the meantime he had been sent to Sultanpur to his sister's village and was there put in charge of the state granary. His inward struggle reached a crisis when he was charged with recklessly giving away the grain. An enquiry was conducted, accounts were scrutinised and the grain was re-weighed. It showed a balance in favour of the Guru. Vindicated he tendered his resignation and decided to commit himself fully to spreading the message of God.

The first utterance of Nanak as he embarked on his mission was that there is no Hindu and no Mussal man. While he wanted the Hindu to be a good Hindu and the Muslim to be a good Muslim, he wanted the man to be a good human being and preached the concept of one God (Ek Onkar).

His message was a simple one. He preached universal brotherhood under the fatherhood of God. He laid stress on the performance of duty. One must work for the good of all, and all must work and secure the good of each member of society. He sought to bring man back to the path of true and purified religion. He preached that: "Truth is the highest virtue, but higher still is truthful living."

To spread his message he undertook arduous and extensive tours in the north, south, east and west and visited important centres of Hindus, Muslims, Buddhists, Jains, Suffis, Jogis and other religions and met people of different races, tribes and diverse cultures.

Guru Nanak's life can be divided into three periods on the basis of his activities. The first period covers his childhood and early manhood, mostly spent in meditation; the second period was spent in travelling; and the last period was that of relatively settled life at Kartarpur (Kartar = God, pur = place) where he lived the life of an ordinary farmer.

The network of centres that Guru Nanak founded contained communities of inspired disciples, which in turn became the body of the Sikh faith which he called 'Sangat'. He established Sikh communities all over India and outside India in Ceylon, Tibet and the Middle East.

He emphasised the need for religious and social discipline. The Japji, Rehras and Kirtan Sohila were fixed as morning, evening and night prayers. He himself worked in his fields, and his disciples were advised and encouraged to have regular daily labour, to have normal relationships with their families and to give some of their income to good causes. His three golden rules are:

1 Naam Japo, meditate on God's name
2 Kirt kero, earn an honest living, and
3 Wand Chhako, share your earnings with the needy.

He also laid the foundation for Guru Ka langar (community kitchen). All worked for their living and gave a part of their earnings for the community kitchen. All the people, Muslim or Hindu, king or pauper, brahmin or low caste, had to sit together in the langar as they ate their meals.

The birthday of Guru Nanak is one of the most important festivals in the Sikh calendar.

Martyrdom of Guru Teg Bahadur

Guru Teg Bahadur was the ninth guru of the Sikhs and son of Guru Hargobind, the sixth guru. He toured the whole of the Punjab, Delhi, Eastern India and Assam preaching the message of the fatherhood of God and the brotherhood of man, as it was preached by Guru Nanak. The Mughal ruler of the time was Aurangzeb who was actively using the machinery of state to quicken the process of Islamisation amongst his subjects, who were mainly Hindus. Many Hindu schools were closed, temples demolished, and mosques built on the sites. Taxes were imposed on non-Muslims when visiting their own holy places, and Jazia, another tax, was imposed on all non-Muslims. Those who could not pay were forcibly converted.

A group of Hindu brahmins (priests) under the leadership of Kirpa Ram came from Kashmir with the news that the ruler of that place was forcibly converting people by breaking their sacred threads and wiping their marks off their foreheads – two important signs of the high-caste Hindu. They said that they had heard about Guru Teg Bahadur as their only saviour and had come to seek his help.

When the Guru heard this tale of oppression, he is said to have remarked that this situation could only be relieved through the sacrifice of a holy person. His nine-year-old son, Gobind Rai, who later became the tenth guru, remarked, "Who is holier than you to make this sacrifice, Father?" At this point, Guru Teg Bahadur told the Kashmiri brahmins to go back to their place and tell the ruler that they would change their faith only if Guru Teg Bahadur became a convert. The consequences were inevitable.

Guru Teg Bahadur's martyrdom is seen by the Sikhs not only as the act of a man accepting death for his own beliefs, but also on behalf of another religion and for the promotion of religious liberty as a principle.

Guru Teg Bahadur is truly a saviour and model for people of all religions the world over.

Guru Gobind Singh composed these verses about his father's sacrifice:

'To preserve their caste marks and sacred threads,
Did he in the dark age perform the supreme sacrifice.
He went to the utmost limit to help the saintly,
He gave his head but never cried in pain.'

The Sikhs have now built a Gurdwara at the place of execution. This martyrdom day is celebrated with great fervour and enthusiasm in Delhi, with a procession taking place one day before the event. Celebrations are held in the Gurdwaras wherever the Sikhs are, on the actual day in India and on the nearest Sunday in the West. They consist of hymn singing, discourses, lectures and sacred food.

Guru Gobind Singh

Guru Gobind Singh was the tenth Guru of the Sikhs. He was born at Patna in the Bihar state of India on 22 December, 1666. The language of the area had a great impact upon his poetry, although he studied not only the Bihari language but also Sanskrit, Persian and Arabic.

As a child he used to have mock battles with other children on the banks of the Ganges and was noted as a great marksman whose arrows never missed the target. At the age of seven he went to Anandpur in Punjab where arrangements were made for his further study of languages. He also learnt archery and swordsmanship.

He became Guru at the age of nine after the martyrdom of Guru Teg Bahadur, and began to consolidate his position as the spiritual head of the community. He lived at Paonta on the banks of the Yamna from 1682 to 1686 and engaged himself in literary pursuits. There he composed the Jaap Sahib and other compositions. He directed the translation of several Sanskrit and Persian classics into Brij Bhasha. He had 52 court poets and most of them helped in the translations. He himself wrote a lot of poetry which is compiled in the Dasam Granth.

On Baisakhi Day of 1699, he revealed the Khalsa on the famous occasion when five beloved ones presented themselves at his command. The dramatic presentation is described in the Baisakhi festival entry on page 57.

Guru Gobind Singh revolutionised the passive resistance movement and introduced the concept of Saint Soldier. He provided common worship, common place of pilgrimage, common baptism for all classes and common external appearance. In this way he brought unity among his followers and gave the slogan 'The Khalsa belongs to God, the victory is of God'.

On 7 October, 1708, he called his followers together, placed five paisas and a coconut before the Guru Granth Sahib, the Holy Book, and bowed to it as his successor. He told the congregation to behold Guru Granth Sahib as the living Guru and spiritual guide. He instructed the Sikhs to:

1 Worship only one God
2 Study Guru Granth Sahib as the spirit of the Guru, and
3 Regard the Khalsa as the visible body of the Guru.

"Where there is five," he said, "the Guru will be present." Guru Granth Sahib is the everlasting Guru of the Sikhs.

Guru Gobind Singh's birthday is celebrated throughout the world wherever there is a Sikh community. On this day, his life story is told to the congregation and hymns are sung in his memory.

Buddhism

Buddhism is the great oriental religion founded in India in the sixth century BC by Siddharta Gautama, who is generally known as the Buddha or 'Enlightened One'.

In his first sermon – 'The Turning of the Wheel of Law' – the Buddha expounded the fundamental ideas on which his teaching is based. These are the Four Noble Truths, namely:

- The Noble Truth of Suffering
- The Noble Truth of the Cause of Suffering
- The Noble Truth of the Cessation of Suffering
- The Noble Truth of the path that leads to the Cessation of Suffering.

The cessation of suffering is **'Nirvana'**. For Buddhists, Nirvana is the final goal of all human endeavour. It refers to a state of being in which lust, ignorance, hatred and egoism become extinct and all human qualities are perfected.

Nirvana can be reached by following the Middle Way, which lies between the two extremes of hedonism and ascetic austerities. It is also known as the Noble Eightfold Path and consists of Right View, Right Thought, Right Speech, Right Action, Right Livelihood, Right Effort, Right Mindfulness and Right Concentration.

Traditionally, Buddhists have expressed their faith by taking refuge in the Buddha, his teachings (dhamma) and in the **Sangha** or assembly of Buddhists who, from the very early times, helped to preserve the teachings of Buddha.

Buddhism in the modern world survives in three major forms. The early **Theravada** form is practised in Sri Lanka, Burma, Thailand, Laos and Cambodia. The later **Mahayana** form prevails in China, Vietnam, Japan, Korea and Mongolia. The form of Buddhism which developed in Tibet is often referred to as **Vajrayana** or **Mantrayana.**

Buddhism in the **Theravada** tradition, is primarily a spiritual philosophy and a system of ethics. The goal of the faithful is to achieve Nirvana and this state of spiritual perfection can be achieved through practice of humility, generosity, mercy, absention from violence and self-control.

In the Theravadin tradition, each individual is expected to work out his own salvation. Religion, in Theravada countries, plays an important role in the critical stages of an individual's life-cycle, such as birth, initiation, marriage and death. Monastic institutions are well-established and play an integral part in the life of the community.

Mahayanists regard Gautama Buddha as one manifestation of an eternal, cosmic Buddha who appears at different times in order to make known the **dhamma** or liberating law.

In the Mahayana tradition, the ideal person is the **bodhisattva** who achieves Enlightenment after great striving but defers entering Nirvana in order to serve and save other suffering mortals. As the Bodhisattva ideal developed, so did the pantheon of Buddhas and bodhisattvas who became the objects of faith and devotion. One of the most important Bodhisattvas is **Avalokiteswara** – the embodiment of Compassion, who is believed to reincarnate in the Dalai Lama of Tibet.

The form of Buddhism introduced into Tibet was a synthesis of the Theravada, Mahayana and Hindu Tantric ideas and practices. It became even more complex by absorbing elements of the indigenous **Bon** religion which was a form of nature worship. Tibetan Buddhism is associated with a voluminous body of scriptures, esoteric teachings, ritual and ceremonial. Great importance was given to the role of the teacher or lama.

Buddhist Festivals

Maghapuja or Dharma Day

This festival, also called All Saints' Day, commemorates three events in the Buddha's life, namely the occasion when he took his two chief disciples, the occasion when he recited the rules by which monks should live, and his announcement that he would die in three month's time.

It is usually celebrated in a monastery in the presence of monks.

Mahaparinirvana

The anniversary of the Buddha's death or liberation (mahaparinirvana) is commemorated in all Buddhist countries, although there are different interpretations of the date on which this event is believed to have occurred.

In the Theravadin Buddhist tradition, the Buddha's birth, enlightenment and death are observed on the same day. (These events occur in May/June, although the actual date varies each year.)

A candlelit procession around the temple is the most usual way the laity observe the anniversary of the Buddha's death/liberation in Theravadin Buddhist countries such as Thailand and Sri Lanka.

In Mahayana Buddhist countries such as Japan, the death anniversary of the Buddha is celebrated on the same day every year. In many Zen Buddhist temples, all lights in the great meditation hall are extinguished on this day (also known as Nehar).

The entire congregation meditates and chants from special Buddhist texts and scriptures and finally the lamps are re-lit. This ritual expresses the hope that the teachings of the Buddha will endure for all time.

Higan

The spring and autumn equinoxes are important days in the Japanese calendar. They not only mark the seasonal changes but also symbolise the spiritual transition from the world of Suffering (Samsara) to the world of Enlightenment (Nirvana). Dead friends and relatives are particularly remembered at these times and special ceremonies are held to transfer merit to the departed.

Hana Matsuri

This festival commemorates the Buddha's birthday according to the Zen Buddhist tradition. In Japan, images of the infant Buddha are washed with a special sweet tea made from hydrangea leaves. In large temples great numbers of priests take part in these rituals.

Vaisakhapuja or Vesak

This is the most important festival in the Theravada Buddhist tradition. It commemorates three important events in the Buddha's life, namely his birth, enlightenment and death.

This is a time when people try especially hard to live up to the teachings of the Buddha. Kindness and generosity are two virtues that are particularly emphasised.

In all Theravada Buddhist countries, the festival is marked by much colour and gaiety. Homes are cleaned and decorated for the occasion. People visit temples to make offerings, and statues of the Buddha are washed with scented water. Streets and homes are lit with lanterns, and in Sri Lanka, there are various street entertainments and pageants. In Thailand, the day's celebrations usually come to an end with candle-lit processions around the local temples.

Poson

This festival marks the bringing of Buddhism to Sri Lanka by the missionary Mahinda. The main feature of the celebrations is the Minindu Perahara, when important events in the life of Mahinda are re-enacted.

Kandy Perahara

Kandy Perahara or Asalha Perahara is probably the most spectacular festival day for Sri Lankan Buddhists. This ten-day festival, celebrated in the ancient highland capital of Kandy, has both religious and national significance. From the Temple of the Tooth, a casket containing a sacred tooth relic of the Buddha is paraded in a colourful procession of elephants, dancers and musicians.

Asalhapuja or Dhammacakka

This festival falls on the full moon day of the month of Asalha. It celebrates the first sermon of Buddha and the setting of the Wheel of Truth (Dhammacakka) into the world.

Rains Retreat

The Rains Retreat, which commences on the full moon day in July and extends until October, is observed in all Theravadin Buddhist countries. This is the time of year when monks settle down in a monastery or sheltered place and spend the time in prayer and contemplation. At the end of the retreat, it is customary for the laity to present the monks with new robes.

Kathina

The Kathina ceremony is observed in Thailand during October/November every year. During the week-long celebrations, the King and members of the Thai royal family visit nine monasteries around the country. A Kathina robe is offered in each monastery to the monk nominated by the abbot as the most virtuous one.

The Kathina ceremony is the only calendrical Buddhist festival authorised in the earliest scriptures.

Enlightenment of the Buddha

In Zen temples, there is a period of intense meditation which re-enacts the Buddha's striving for enlightenment.

Jainism

Jainism is one of three major religions that developed in ancient India. It probably had its roots in a strand of the 'renouncer' tradition, which appeared in India around the 8th century BCE as a reaction against the highly ritualistic form of Brahmanical Hinduism. The beliefs that form the core of Jainism, however, were given shape in the 6th century BCE by Vardhamana Mahavira, a contemporary of the Buddha.

Legend has it that Mahavira, the son of a warrior chieftan, left his home at the age of thirty in search of salvation from the cycle of birth, death and rebirth. After twelve years of wandering, during which time he practised rigorous austerities, he found enlightenment and became 'a perfect soul' or 'conqueror' – **Jina.** Mahavira gained royal patronage and popular support for his new doctrine of salvation and his followers came to be known as **Jainas** or 'Followers of the Conqueror'. He is believed to have died at the age of seventy-two by the rite of **'sallekhana'** or voluntary self-starvation.

Jainism is essentially an atheistic, ascetic discipline which places great emphasis on physical austerities and self-inflicted pain as a means of freeing oneself from the cycle of birth and death. Intentions and actions in this life determine the nature and quality of the next. The cycle of birth and rebirth is broken only when perfection is reached.

According to Jain cosmography, the universe is eternal and moves through a continuous cycle of progress and decline. Sin and sorrow in their milder forms began to appear in the third period and the need for spiritual guidance was felt. Twenty-four **'Tirthankaras'** – 'Ford builders' or 'Enlightened souls' appeared on earth to preach the Jain doctrines. The last of the Tirthankaras was Mahavira.

The Jains believe that the entire universe is full of life and that even the four elements – earth, water, air and fire – are animated by souls. The Jain code of ethics is directed towards the avoidance of injury to any living being.

The principle of **ahimsa** or the avoidance of violence or injury, expresses itself in various ways. Vegetarianism is one practice that continues to endure among Jains.

Monks and ascetics cover their mouths with a small mask in order to preserve the life of the air itself and to avoid breathing in any of the small insects of the air.

Image worship was introduced at an early stage in the history of Jainism. The construction of shrines and temples came to be regarded as a pious act and many of these temples are remarkable for their rich and intricate ornamentation. Although Mahavira rejected the authority of the Hindu sacred texts, the efficacy of ritual sacrifice and the underlying rationale of the Hindu caste system, temple worship amongst the Jains has been greatly influenced by Hindu practices. Jain temples contain images of the Tirthankaras as well as many of the Hindu gods, and it is customary to chant hymns of praise and sacred formulae as well as to make offerings of fruits, flowers and grain.

Around 300 BCE, the Jaina monastic community was split into two main sects: the **'Digambaras'** or 'sky-clad' who believed in total reincarnation of all material things, including articles of clothing, and the **'Swetambaras'** who are usually clad in white cotton garments. A seventeenth century offshoot of the Swetambaras, the **Sthanakvasis,** allow little compromise over the rigorous discipline laid down in the Jain scriptures and tend to reject image worship and other practices that have crept into the religion over time.

Jain Festivals

Principal Jain festivals are linked to major events in the lives of the Tirthankaras, particularly Rishabha (the first Tirthankara), Mahavira and his immediate predecessor, Parshva. The birthdate and death/liberation date of Mahavira, in the months of Chaitra (March/April) and Karttika (October/November) respectively, are widely celebrated by all Jain communities.

Monthly fast dates are also observed, the most significant of these being **Akshayatrtiya** (the immmortal third), celebrated in the month of Vaisakha (April/May) and commemorating the first giving of alms to Rishabha, the first Tirthankara.

Paryushana

This is the most important Jain festival. It is celebrated for eight days by Swetambaras or ten days by Digambaras, in the month of Bhadrapada (August/September). During this period, lay persons perform austerities on the ascetic model. On the final day of Paryushana (Samvatsari), it is customary for individuals to confess their transgressions of the past year and letters are written and visits paid for the purpose of asking and extending forgiveness.

The Baha'i Faith

The Baha'i faith was founded in the late 1850s by Mirza Hussain Ali. He called himself Baha'u'llah or 'Glory of God' and after several mystical experiences believed he was a Manifestation of God, sent to interpret the divine message for a new era. The primary sources of Baha'i doctrine and practice are the writings of Baha'u'llah and the authorised interpretations of these by his successors.

The Baha'i faith is founded upon a belief in an all-powerful omniscient Being who created the entire universe. Man has always been aware of a mysterious power in the universe and has developed complex, abstract ideas about the first cause through which creation came into being. However, Baha'i teachings declare that the essential nature of God is beyond human comprehension except through the medium of 'Manifestations' or highly spiritual individuals who appeared at various periods in human history, charged with a messianic mission. Baha'u'llah is believed to be the Manifestation of God for the present age. Previous Manifestations include Abraham, Moses, Krishna, Zoroaster, the Buddha, Jesus Christ, Mohammed and the Bab, a powerful spiritual leader who inspired Baha'u'llah. The Baha'is believe that Baha'u'llah will be succeeded in future ages by other Manifestations who build upon the teachings of their predecessors but adapt their mission to the circumstances.

The core of Baha'i theology is 'evolution in time and unity in the present hour'. All phenomena including the revelations of God, are subject to the process of evolution. World unity is the last stage in the evolution of mankind and the purpose of the Baha'i faith is to foster this unity.

Baha'u'llah categorically rejected the notion of sin and evil. In Baha'i eschatology, heaven and hell are spiritual states rather than physical entities. Heaven is the state of perfection and harmony with God's will; hell is the absence of such harmony.

The Baha'i religion is characterised by the total absence of public rituals or sacraments. However, followers of the faith are expected to observe certain rituals in the course of their daily lives. An important aspect of daily worship are the obligatory prayers which must be recited at prescribed times during the day. Practising Baha'is are also expected to read daily from the writings of the Bab and Baha'u'llah. Time must also be set aside each day for meditation and quiet contemplation.

The religious duties of a Baha'i also include assembling on the first day of each month in the Baha'i calendar in the home of a member of the community to celebrate the Feast of the Nineteenth Day. The occasion is a form of social exchange where congregational worship and the sharing of food assume great symbolic significance.

The nineteenth month of the Baha'i calendar is particularly important. Followers of the faith are expected to fast from dawn to sunset throughout the month.

Important Anniversaries and Holy Days

Baha'i New Year

March 21 is the first day of the Baha'i year, and is a time for rejoicing, as it also signals the end of the fast. It begins at sunset on 20 March, and can take any form, provided there are a few prayers, and then there can be dancing, a musical performance or other celebrations.

The First Day of Ridvan

This is the most important day in the Baha'i year. After the death of the Bab (the Gate), his followers were known as the Babis, and they gradually came to look upon one of his followers, Baha'u'llah, as their leader. The Muslim authorities decided to kill off the movement altogether by sending the leader into exile to a series of countries belonging to the Ottoman Empire. The first stage of his exile was in Baghdad, in what is now Iraq, but they gave no indication at that time as to his next destination. Meanwhile, he camped in the open, in large tents in a public park, accompanied by an ever-growing crowd of Babis who wanted to be with him until the last possible moment. They were grieving at the imminent parting, but at some time during their stay in the park, he informed them that he was the one promised to them by the Bab, as 'Him whom God shall make manifest', and the weeping changed to ecstasy and joy, as everyone realised that they had been privileged to meet the Promised One, even if only briefly before they would lose him.

In their joy they called the park 'the garden of Paradise', which is equivalent to Rivdan, in the Persian language. This was the momentous birth of the Baha'i Faith, the Revelation given to Baha'u'llah (the Glory of God), during his incarceration in a filthy dungeon some years previously, but which he kept secret until this time of the Ridvan festival. His advent is the culmination of all the promises of all religions, and there are many passages in all the Holy Books which relate to this time as being the time of the reconciliation of all faiths, and of universal peace as man comes to maturity. The time of prophecy is over, and the age of fulfilment begins. The founders of all previous faiths are revered as 'sitting on the same throne', and thus unity can become a reality.

On this day, throughout the world, the believers in every town, city or village, meet to celebrate and to hold their annual elections for the nine members of their community to serve on the local spiritual assembly for one year. No canvassing is allowed, and the balloting is secret, resting solely upon the good character and spirituality of those elected.

Ninth Day of Ridvan

On the ninth day of Ridvan, the family of Baha'u'llah finished their preparations for the journey, and joined him. Prayers are said, and Baha'i history books may be read, and so on.

Twelfth Day of Ridvan

On the twelfth day of Ridvan, Baha'u'llah and his family left to go over the mountains, and through the winter snows, to the shores of the Black Sea, going on by boat and landing at Constantinople; then via Adrianople to Gallipoli, and by sea to Alexandria. Finally, they were shipped to Akka, where he was confined to the old prison barracks, in a room looking out over the sea, with not a green tree in sight. The Israelis have nowadays given this room to the Baha'is, where it is visited by Baha'i pilgrims from around the world, but nobody else may go there.

Declaration of the Bab

A spiritual seeker, Mullah Husayn, arrived at the town of Shiraz, and was met by a young siyyid (a direct descendant of the prophet Mohammed) wearing a green turban, who seemed to have been expecting him, and invited the traveller to his home. They spent the evening in prayer, and eventually the host revealed to his guest that all the signs given to him by his teacher, and the conditions laid down, were fulfilled in the young siyyid, as being the one whose advent all the wise people of Islam awaited. He called himself the Bab (Gate), and told Mullah Husayn that henceforth he would be known as the Bab-ul-Bab, which meant the Gate of the Gate.

The Bab further declared, "This night, this very hour, shall, in the years to come, be regarded as one of the greatest festivals." The very hour registered on the clock was two hours and eleven minutes after sunset in the year 1844. The Bab cautioned his visitor to tell nobody about this meeting, for seventeen other souls should spontaneously arise and find him, and together they would all constitute the 'Nineteen Letters of the Living', to bring the good news to all peoples. The Bab also said his sole purpose was to prepare the world for the Promised One of all faiths and the scriptural prophecies of the past, and he said, "I am but a ring upon his finger." The Baha'i Era dates from that year 1844 in the Western calendar. The Baha'is celebrate the day with joy, and send cards.

Ascension of Baha'u'llah

After imprisonment in Akka for two years in the old barracks, from which he wrote letters to the ruling monarchs and leaders of the world, Baha'u'llah, his son Abdu'l-Baha (Servant of the Glory) and his family were moved to various locations, and Baha'u'llah was eventually given complete freedom, and enjoyed the great esteem of many people.

He died peacefully. He lies buried in a mansion in Bahji, surrounded by a beautiful garden, laid out in such a way as to symbolise the order in the world of the future. Pilgrims to the Baha'i shrines in Israel, visit the tomb to pray there. They come from all quarters of the globe.

The Martyrdom of the Bab

During all the years of his brief Ministry from the age of 25 to 31, the Bab was hounded and persecuted by the divines of the prevailing state religion, and consigned to bleak prisons in obscure parts of Iran, in the hope that he and his teachings would be forgotten. Eventually he was condemned to death, and the story of his execution is most extraordinary and worth telling.

One of his disciples begged to be allowed to share his fate, and this wish was granted. On the eve of his execution, the leader of the execution squad, a Christian, came to see the prisoner, and confessed to him that he did not personally harbour any grudge against him and did not want to kill him. The Bab said, "If your intention be sincere, the Almighty is surely able to relieve you of your perplexity."

When the hour came, the Bab and his disciple were suspended, face to face, by ropes passing under their armpits, from a prominent pillar in the barrack square of Tabriz. Thousands of people stood on the walls, jeering. An Armenian firing squad lined up and fired, and when the smoke cleared, the Bab had gone, but his disciple was standing against the wall, unhurt. Only the ropes had been severed, and the Bab was found back in his cell, dictating notes to a secretary. The soldiers were so shaken by the 'miracle' that they all refused to try again. In due course, a new regiment was called in and the prisoners again tied up.

The Bab addressed the crowds in these words, "Had you believed in me, every one of you would have followed the example of this youth, who stood in rank above most of you, and would have willingly sacrificed himself in my path. The day will come when you will have recognised me; that day I shall have ceased to be with you." And so they fired again and this time the bodies were riddled with bullets, but the faces little marred. The bodies were eventually rescued from a moat outside the town into which they had been thrown, and were hidden by faithful believers until, years later, the remains were interred on Mount Carmel in Israel, beneath the lovely golden-domed building known as the Queen of Carmel. The execution was at noon and at that time all over the world, the Baha'is read special prayers for the occasion, turning to stand in the direction of Haifa. This is a 'no-work' day.

The Birthday of the Bab

He was born in 1819 in Shiras, Persia. As his father died when he was still a baby, he was brought up by a maternal uncle. One day he was sent home from school because his teacher considered that there was nothing more he could teach him. The uncle thought the child must have behaved badly, but the teacher said that the pupil knew more than he did – the fact being that he had innate knowledge. The Bab was a direct descendant of the Prophet Mohammed, and therefore was entitled to wear the traditional green turban. He has been described as being sweet and gentle mannered, of noble character, and great personal beauty. He was trained in commerce, and was known for his fair dealings.

The believers celebrate this event with reverence and joy, in community gatherings.

The Birthday of Baha'u'llah

He was born before sunrise, in the year 1817, of a wealthy family, and his father was a Minister of State at the court of Shah. Upon his death when his son was 22 years old, the post was offered to the young man, who turned it down, and the Prime Minister said, "But I am convinced that he is destined for some lofty career..." Baha'u'llah accepted the mission of the Bab and accordingly suffered the fate of thousands of those who thought as he did, and was imprisoned under awful conditions. However, it was in the dungeon that he experienced his revelation.

His birthday is celebrated with parties as well as the community gathering. Gifts are given, and cards sent to absent friends overseas.

Day of the Covenant

An anniversary, not a holy day. When Baha'u'llah died, he left a will and testament decreeing that the believers should turn to his eldest son, whom he referred to as the 'Most Great Branch', the 'Branch from the Ancient Root', and 'The Master', and the 'Centre of His Covenant'. It ensured that there should be no divergence of opinion among the believers and no split in the community, as all turned to Abdu'l-Baha for guidance. In his turn, Abdu'l-Baha appointed his eldest grandson to be the sole interpreter of his words and those of Baha'u'llah. The Guardian, as he was called, left provision for the election of the Universal House of Justice, which Abdu'l-Baha had outlined and said, "Whatever they say is of God. Whoever obeys them has obeyed God, and whoever has disobeyed them has disobeyed God." Abdu'l-Baha is known as the Centre of the Covenant, and as the perfect exemplar of the faith.

Ascension of Abdu'l-Baha

In 1921, in Haifa, Israel (then Palestine), Abdu'l-Baha suffered years of imprisonment, before being set free by the Young Turks Rising, after which he travelled to the West, including Britain, where he met with many important people who flocked to see him and discuss various problems with him. At home in Palestine he was known as the 'father of the poor'. He was knighted by the British Government for saving the people from famine during the First World War, by having saved up grain in anticipation of such an event. Many thousands of mourners came together for his funeral, representing all levels of society, including the High Commissioner, Sir Herbert Samuel, the Governor of Jerusalem, the Consuls of various countries, the heads of the various religious communities, Jews, Christians, Muslims, Druzes, Egyptians, Greeks. The representatives of the Jews, Christians and Muslims raised their voices in eulogy and regret.

"So united were they in their acclamation of him as the wise educator and reconciler of the human race in this perplexed and sorrowful age, that there seemed to be nothing left for the Baha'is to say."
– Lady Blomfield

His funeral was truly the uniting of many peoples of all races, creeds and colours. He was interred in the shrine on Mount Carmel. The believers commemorate the event at about 1.30 a.m.

National, Secular and Folk Festivals – of special interest

Ganjitsu – Japanese New Year

New Year's Day is celebrated with a morning visit to a shrine or temple. A family dinner, the Osechi, is eaten. This is cooked on New Year's Eve and placed in the jyubaker or special box. Included with the dinner is a traditional Japanese rice cake containing Omochi and Zoni.

An ancient game, called hajoita, is played for Japanese pennies. The bats used for the game have colourful paintings on one side.

Parents 'spoil' their children a little on this day with cash gifts or otoshidama.

Setsubon – Japanese Spring Festival

Special rituals are conducted to drive out evil spirits. A wooden rice measure containing beans is placed on the shrine by the head of the family household. As darkness falls, the beans are scattered around all the entrances of the house and in the dark corners. A small charm is then placed over each entrance to prevent the evil spirits from sneaking into the house.

Tu B'Shevat

This marks the end of the heavy rain season in Israel and commemorates the New Year for Trees.

This minor festival has received new significance with the establishment of the modern state of Israel, where young children are encouraged to plant trees in celebration.

Jewish children may attend school on this day.

Chinese New Year

New Year's Day is the most important event in the Chinese calendar and marks the beginning of the first lunar month. The festivities generally last for two or three weeks, though the first week tends to be the most important.

A week before the New Year, the family will honour the kitchen god, and he then reports to heaven on their conduct. While he is away the house must be thoroughly cleaned, debts should be paid, all food should be prepared, and the home decorated with flowers such as peach blossoms or jonquils. The kitchen god returns on New Year's Eve and fire crackers are let off.

For the New Year, people wear new clothes to represent the discarding of the old year and its misfortunes. Visits are made to relatives and friends with gifts of food and drink. Traditional foods include cakes made from rice flour or sesame seeds, and kumquats which signify prosperity. The usual greeting to be heard at New Year is, in Cantonese (the most widely spoken Chinese dialect in Britain), "Kung hay fat choy" (pronounced like "Goong hay fut choy") meaning "May you prosper". Another important custom at this time is the giving of money in red paper packets by married couples to unmarried relatives, friends and children. In Cantonese these are called 'laisee' or 'hungpow' and are believed to bring luck.

The Lantern Festival on the first full moon of the New Year marks the end of the festivities. It celebrates the return of light, the coming of spring and the beginning of the growing season. Strings of lanterns of all shapes, sizes and colours are hung out to decorate homes and public places. Besides the family celebrations there are also colourful community events, of which the most important are the dragon and lion dances.

A lion dance can be seen at New Year in London's Chinatown. The 'two-man' pantomime lion dances through the streets to the sound of gongs and drums and reaches up to take money in red packets hung outside shops. It is believed that to give the lion money and food, such as kumquats and lettuce, will bring the establishment good fortune.

1997 is the year of the Ox; 1998 – the Tiger; 1999 – the Hare; 2000 – the Dragon; and 2001 – the Snake.

Losar – The Tibetan New Year

Losar is a three-day festival. On the first day, celebrations are restricted mainly to the family. On the second and third days, visits and gifts are exchanged with friends and relatives.

Houses are whitewashed and thoroughly cleaned, people wear new clothes and special food is prepared. Good luck symbols such as dried ears of corn are placed in the house, and dishes of water and dough models called 'torna' are placed in household shrines along with other offerings.

People visit monasteries to make offerings and Buddhist monks conduct special religious ceremonies. A number of rituals are performed to drive away evil spirits and alms are given to the poor. There is also much merry-making with feasts, dancing and archery competitions.

1997 is the year 2124 in the Tibetan Buddhist calendar; 2001 is the year 2128.

Monlam Chenmo

Monlam Chenmo or the Great Prayer Festival is celebrated in Tibet from the fourth day of the New Year until the 25th day. The fifteenth day – Chonga Chopa – is particularly spectacular. Scenes from the Buddha's life are sculpted in butter and coloured with vegetable dyes. The visual displays are accompanied by puppet shows and other street celebrations.

Hina Matsuri

Hina Matsuri, the Japanese Dolls' Festival, was originally celebrated as the Girls' Festival.

A display of beautiful dolls is the main feature of the celebrations. The ceremonial dolls are usually handed from generation to generation within a family, and are placed on display in the best room of the house. In addition to the dolls, exquisitely crafted miniature household articles are also displayed. The dolls most highly valued are the 'Daini-Sana' which represent the Emperor and Empress, both dressed in elaborate court attire. When the festival (3 March) is over, the articles are carefully packed away and stored until the next year.

April Fool's Day

All Fool's Day – the 'fun' day when people are tricked by others or sent on silly errands, is observed in many countries in Europe and Asia.

The origin of these practices is obscure. One explanation as to why it is so widespread is that 1 April marked the end of the spring equinox, when celebrations were held to mark the period when the sun's rays fall vertically on the equator, and day and night are of equal length all over the earth.

According to some British historians, 1 April marks the end of the New Year celebrations in the old calendar when New Year's Day was 25 March. Yet another explanation offered is that it is a remnant of an old Celtic rite.

Qingming Festival

Qingming (pronounced 'Chingming'), or the Chinese Tomb-sweeping Festival, is not fixed by the lunar calendar, but occurs on the day the sun's longitude passes fifteen degrees at the start of one of the 24 sections of the solar year.

From early in the morning people visit their ancestors' shrines and tombs, carrying with them offerings of incense, joss paper and food cooked specially for the dead. Family members sweep the tombs of their loved ones, clear the ground of weeds, plant a new tree and repaint faded inscriptions on the tombstone. Joss paper is distributed around the tombs as a mark of their visit. Imitation paper money or gold, and paper clothes may be burnt as sacrificial gifts for the ancestors.

The festival is not usually celebrated in Britain, though many overseas Chinese return home sometimes for New Year and Qingming.

Sinhala and Tamil New Year's Day

This is a time of great merrymaking, and it is customary for people to be lavish in their hospitality on this day. Special sweetmeats and delicacies are prepared and people dress in their finery to participate in the various celebrations.

In Sri Lanka, New Year's Eve is also celebrated as a public holiday.

Songkrar Day

This is also celebrated as the Thai New Year. The main feature of the celebrations is the water festival. Many colourful spectacles such as boat races, parades, pageants and the appearance of the Songkrar Princess on a splendidly caparisoned wooden horse, are also associated with this festival.

On the last day of the festival, a drum and bell are simultaneously sounded three times in temples all over the land. As the vibrations die away the festivities come to an end for another year.

For the past 50 years or so, Thai New Year has been celebrated on 31 December, although there remains an historic link with old April celebrations.

May 1

May Day is an old folk festival which later acquired religious significance, but like many other festivals its origins are disputed. According to one legend, it stems from the Roman Festival to Maia, the mother of Mercury, in whose honour sacrifices were made on the first day of her month, accompanied by considerable merrymaking.

May Day celebrations are also associated with the beneficent qualities ascribed to tree spirits. This explanation suggests that May Day festivities are relics of the ancient custom of tree worship.

In medieval England, May Day was a public holiday when most villages arranged processions, with all those participating carrying green boughs of sycamore and hawthorn. The most conspicuous element in the procession would be the Maypole – a young tall tree, stripped of its branches and decorated with garlands of flowers and ribbons.

May Day celebrations did not find favour with the Church and devout Christians for a long time, and when Oliver Cromwell came to power all festivities were forbidden. It was only later when Charles II came to the throne that the customary merrymaking associated with this folk festival was revived.

Towards the end of the nineteenth century, 1 May became known as Labour Day, and is commemorated in many parts of the world with military parades and political rallies.

Boys' Festival

Since World War Two, 5 May has been designated a national holiday in Japan and is known as Kodomono Hi or Children's Day.

Paper or cloth streamers in the shape of a carp are hoisted on a wooden pole in the yard or garden. Several legends account for the choice of the carp, the most popular being based on the fact that this fish has great energy, power and determination to overcome obstacles and is therefore a fitting example for young boys.

This day is as much a day of festivity for small boys as 3 March is for girls in Japan.

Dragon Boat Festival

Duan Yang, or the Dragon Boat Festival, is celebrated on the fifth day of the fifth lunar month. It commemorates the suicide by drowning in 279 BC of Qu Yuan, a famous poet and high-ranking official. Legend has it that the peasants took out their dragon boats and rushed to save him, but in vain. In order to prevent the fish eating his body, they threw rice dumplings wrapped in bamboo leaves into the river. These dumplings are still made and eaten during the festival.

It also became the custom to hold races between dragon boats. These are very long narrow rowing boats, brightly painted like dragons with plenty of red and gold and with a dragon's head at the prow. They are usually manned by rival crews from neighbouring villages. The races take place accompanied by men waving flags and the noise of beating gongs. Later, in the evening, the boats parade along the water bedecked with colourful lanterns.

The races are not held in Britain, but there is a spectacular international race held in Hong Kong.

Obon

A four-day festival celebrated in Japan to pay respect to the spirits of dead ancestors. Legend has it that the Buddha rescued the mother of one of his disciples on this day after she had been sent to one of the hells. Graves are cleaned and decorated with flowers. Incense is lit and prayers offered. The spirits of the dead are invited to return home and hemp reeds are burned to light the way. Special food is prepared for the honoured guests.

At the end of Obon, the Bon-Odori dances take place. This is a simple folk dance performed to the accompaniment of songs and drum beats.

Onam

Onam is celebrated as a harvest festival by people of all faiths in Kerala – the state at the south-western tip of India.

According to legend, Kerala was once ruled by the benevolent King Mahabali. The gods, jealous of his popularity, determined to teach him a lesson. Thus Vishnu – one of the Holy Trinity in the Hindu pantheon – appeared in the guise of a dwarf brahmin and begged the King for as much land as he could cover in three paces. The King immediately agreed, and in fact begged the Brahmin to take more land. Vishnu, however, could not be tempted and proceeded to measure out the three paces. The first step he took covered the heavens and the second the entire earth. For the third step, he placed his foot on the bowed head of the King, who had by this time realised the true identity of the dwarf Brahmin, and pushed him into the earth, first granting him the wish of being allowed to return once a year to visit his subjects.

On this day, therefore, people dress up in new clothes and decorate their homes with beautiful flower arrangements. A grand feast is prepared and food is distributed to the brahmins and to the poor and needy.

The festivities in the state are also marked by boat races. The normally quiet backwaters of Kerala are transformed as people line the banks along the route to cheer their favourite team. The celebrations are brought to an end with firework displays.

The festival is held in August/September. The exact date is available, near to the time, on a year-by-year basis.

Mid-Autumn Festival

Zhong Qiu, the Chinese Mid-Autumn or Moon Festival, is held on the fifteenth day of the eighth month, which in a lunar month is the day of, or day before, the full moon. It is one of the major festivals, and traditionally incense is burned and offerings of fruit such as melons, pomegranates, grapes and peaches together with mooncakes are made to the moon goddess and to the hare which lives in the moon.

The mooncakes commemorate an uprising against the Mongols in the fourteenth century when the call to revolt was written on pieces of paper embedded in the cakes. They are made of a pastry filled with bean paste or lotus seeds, and often contain solid duck egg yolks to represent the moon.

The festivities may include lion dances, and in the evening children form parades carrying multi-coloured lanterns. These may be made in many shapes from cars and planes to traditional animals such as the symbolic carp or mandarin ducks.

Mooncakes and lanterns are sold around this time in London's Chinatown, and there is usually a lion dance.

Chong Yang Festival

Chong Yang, the ninth day of the ninth moon, also called Double Nine, is a Chinese festival commemorating an incident which is believed to have taken place on this day.

According to the legend, there were two friends who travelled together for many years pursuing their studies. One day, one of them had a premonition that on the ninth day of the ninth moon, the household of his friend would meet with a grave disaster. It could be avoided if the family left their home for the day and took refuge in the hills.

The friend did as he was advised and did

not return home with his family until nightfall. On their return, they discovered that during their absence all the domestic animals had perished mysteriously. The same fate would have overtaken the family had they not fled to the hills. Since then, it has become customary for Chinese people to climb hills, towers and pagodas on Double Nine, which is also called the Day of Ascending Heights.

Hallowe'en

An ancient Celtic celebration which is a mixture of pagan ideas, folklore and religion, celebrating the end of the Celtic year. Witches and evil spirits have to be driven away before the beginning of the new year. Bonfires and the ceremonial extinguishing of fire and lights symbolise the end of the year. Many games and superstitions are associated with it.

Guy Fawkes Day

Guy Fawkes Day is celebrated all over Britain on 5 November. On this day in 1605, a conspirator called Guy Fawkes tried to blow up King James I of England and his Parliament.

The nationwide celebrations feature fireworks and bonfires on which effigies of Guy Fawkes are burnt. These effigies are usually made by children who beg passers-by on the streets for 'a penny for the guy'.

Since the abortive plot of 1605, the vaults of the House of Lords are always searched by the sovereign's bodyguard – the Yeomen of the Guard – before the State Opening of Parliament.

The Guy Fawkes celebrations might have faded out, had not William of Orange landed at Torbay on the very day, rekindling Protestant emotions. Both events were commemorated in a state service bound up with the Church of England Prayer Book, until the services were abrogated by Queen Victoria in 1859.

Thanksgiving

Thanksgiving Day was first celebrated in America by the Pilgrim Fathers to mark their gratitude for a good harvest in their first year of settlement in a new land. The American celebration is an adaptation of Lammas Day (Loaf Mass, August 1) which was celebrated in Britain only if there was an abundant harvest. Loaves of bread made from the successful wheat crop were brought to Mass as a token of thanksgiving.

Abraham Lincoln was the first US President to declare Thanksgiving as a national festival and he set the date as the last Thursday in November. This was later changed by President Roosevelt to the fourth Thursday in November.

Roast turkey and pumpkin pie are the main elements of the traditional Thanksgiving meal. The latter has close links with the native American Indians who cultivated the vegetable, and which they, in all probability, shared with the English settlers.

Dates of Major Festivals and Holy Days

Hindu Festival Dates

	1997	1998	1999	2000	2001
Lohri	12 Jan	13 Jan	13 Jan	13 Jan	13 Jan
Makara Sankrant/Pongal	13 Jan	14 Jan	14 Jan	14 Jan	13 Jan
Vasanta/Basant Panchami	11 Feb	1 Feb	22 Jan	10 Feb	29 Jan
Mahasivaratri	7 Mar	25 Feb	15 Feb	4 Mar	21 Feb
Holi	24 Mar	14 Mar	3 Mar	21 Mar	10 Mar
Ramnavami	16 Apr	5 Apr	25 Mar	12 Apr	2 Apr
Vaisakhi/Baisakhi	13 Apr	13 Apr	14 Apr	13 Apr	13 Apr
Tamil New Year / Sinhala New Year	13 Apr	13 Apr	13 Apr	13 Apr	13 Apr
Vishu	14 Apr	14 Apr	14 Apr	14 Apr	14 Apr
Rakshabandhan	18 Aug	8 Aug	26 Aug	15 Aug	4 Aug
Janmashtami	24 Aug	14 Aug	2 Sep	22 Aug	12 Aug
Ganesh Chaturthi	6 Sep	26 Aug	13 Sep	1 Sep	22 Aug
Dassera	11 Oct	1 Oct	19 Oct	7 Oct	26 Oct
Karva Chauth	19 Oct	8 Oct	27 Oct	16 Oct	4 Nov
Deepawali/Diwali	30 Oct	19 Oct	7 Nov	26 Oct	14 Nov

Muslim Festival Dates

	1997	1998	1999	2000
Lailat-ul-Qadr	4 Feb	25 Jan	14 Jan	3 Jan
Eid-ul-Fitr	9 Feb	30 Jan	19 Jan	8 Jan
Eid-ul-Adha	18 Apr	7 Apr	28 Mar	16 Mar
Hijrat (New Year)	(1418)	(1419)	(1420)	(1421)
Muharram	8 May	28 Apr	17 Apr	6 Apr
Ashuraa	17 May	7 May	26 Apr	15 Apr
Milad-un-Nabi	17 Jul	7 Jun	26 Jun	15 Jun
Shab-e-Miraj	26 Nov	16 Nov	4 Nov	24 Oct
Shab-e-Barat	14 Dec	3 Dec	22 Nov	10 Nov
Ramadhan 1st	10 Jan 31 Dec	20 Dec	9 Dec	27 Nov

Note: The Muslim Festival Dates for 2001 will not be available until near that time (see page 8).

Jewish Holy Days – Dates

	1997	1998	1999	2000	2001
Passover (Pesach)					
1st Day	22 Apr	11 Apr	1 Apr	20 Apr	8 Apr
2nd Day	23 Apr	12 Apr	2 Apr	21 Apr	9 Apr
7th Day	28 Apr	17 Apr	7 Apr	26 Apr	14 Apr
8th Day	29 Apr	18 Apr	8 Apr	27 Apr	15 Apr
Pentecost (Shavuot)					
1st Day	11 Jun	31 May	21 May	9 Jun	28 May
2nd Day	12 Jun	1 Jun	22 May	10 Jun	29 May
New Year (Rosh Hashanah)					
1st Day	2 Oct	21 Sep	11 Sep	30 Sep	18 Sep
2nd Day	3 Oct	22 Sep	12 Sep	1 Oct	19 Sep
Day of Atonement (Yom Kippur)	11 Oct	30 Sep	20 Sep	9 Oct	27 Sep
Tabernacles (Succot)					
1st Day	16 Oct	5 Oct	25 Sep	14 Oct	2 Oct
2nd Day	17 Oct	6 Oct	26 Sep	15 Oct	3 Oct
8th Day	23 Oct	12 Oct	2 Oct	21 Oct	9 Oct
9th Day (Simchat Torah)	24 Oct	13 Oct	3 Oct	22 Oct	10 Oct

Other Jewish Festivals

Tu B'Shevat	end Jan/early Feb
Lag B'Omer	end Apr/beginning May
Chanucah	8 days commencing on 25th day of Hebrew month of Kislev (Dec)
Purim	14th day of Hebrew month of Adar (Mar/Apr)

Christian Festivals – Dates

	1997	1998	1999	2000	2001
New Year's Day	1 Jan	1 Jan	1 Jan	1 Jan	1 Jan
Epiphany	6 Jan	6 Jan	6 Jan	6 Jan	6 Jan
Christian Unity Week	19–25 Jan	18–24 Jan	17–23 Jan	16–22 Jan	21–27 Jan
St Brigid's Day	1 Feb	1 Feb	1 Feb	1 Feb	1 Feb
Candlemas Day	2 Feb	2 Feb	2 Feb	2 Feb	2 Feb
Shrove Tuesday	11 Feb	24 Feb	16 Feb	7 Mar	27 Feb
Ash Wednesday	12 Feb	25 Feb	17 Feb	8 Mar	28 Feb
St David's Day	1 Mar	1 Mar	1 Mar	1 Mar	1 Mar
St Patrick's Day	17 Mar	17 Mar	17 Mar	17 Mar	17 Mar
Mothering Sunday	9 Mar	22 Mar	14 Mar	9 Apr	25 Mar
Palm Sunday	23 Mar	5 Apr	28 Mar	16 Apr	8 Apr
Good Friday	28 Mar	10 Apr	2 Apr	21 Apr	13 Apr
Holy Saturday	29 Mar	11 Apr	3 Apr	22 Apr	14 Apr
Easter Sunday	30 Mar	12 Apr	4 Apr	23 Apr	15 Apr
St George's Day	23 Apr	23 Apr	23 Apr	23 Apr	23 Apr
Christian Aid Week	12–17 May	10–16 May	9–15 May	14–20 May	13–19 May
Ascension Day	8 May	21 May	13 May	1 Jun	24 May
Pentecost Day (Whit Sunday)	18 May	31 May	23 May	11 Jun	3 Jun
Corpus Christi	29 May	11 Jun	3 Jun	22 Jun	14 Jun
Sts Peter and Paul	29 Jun	29 Jun	29 Jun	29 Jun	29 Jun
Assumption of The Blessed Virgin	15 Aug	15 Aug	15 Aug	15 Aug	15 Aug
Harvest Festival	28 Sep	27 Sep	26 Sep	24 Sep	30 Sep
All Saints' Day	1 Nov	1 Nov	1 Nov	1 Nov	1 Nov
All Souls' Day	2 Nov	2 Nov	2 Nov	2 Nov	2 Nov
First Sunday of Advent	30 Nov	29 Nov	28 Nov	3 Dec	2 Dec
St Andrew's Day	30 Nov	30 Nov	30 Nov	30 Nov	30 Nov
Christmas Day	25 Dec	25 Dec	25 Dec	25 Dec	25 Dec
St Stephen's Day	26 Dec	26 Dec	26 Dec	26 Dec	26 Dec
Boxing Day	26 Dec	26 Dec	27 Dec	26 Dec	26 Dec

Sikh Festivals – Dates

	1997	1998	1999	2000
Basant Panchami	11 Feb	1 Feb	22 Jan	10 Feb
Baisakhi	13 Apr	13 Apr	14 Apr	13 Apr
Martyrdom of Guru Arjan Dev	9 Jun	29 May	17 Jun	5 Jun
Sikh Diwali	30 Oct	19 Oct	7 Nov	26 Oct
Birthday of Guru Nanak	14 Nov	4 Nov	23 Nov	11 Nov
Martyrdom of Guru Teg Bahadur	4 Dec	24 Nov	13 Dec	1 Dec
Birthday of Guru Gobind Singh	15 Jan	25 Dec	—	14 Jan

Note: The Sikh Festival dates for 2001 will not be available until nearer that time (see page 8).

Buddhist Festivals – Dates

	1997	1998	1999	2000	2001
Maghapuja	21 Feb	11 Feb	2 Mar	19 Feb	8 Feb
Mahaparinirvana (Death Anniversary of the Buddha)	15 Feb	15 Feb	15 Feb	15 Feb	15 Feb
Birthday of the Buddha (Mahayana tradition)	8 Apr	8 Apr	8 Apr	8 Apr	8 Apr
Vesak (Theravada tradition)	20 May	10 May	30 Apr	18 May	7 May
Poson	20 Jun	10 Jun	28 Jun	16 Jun	6 Jun
Asalhapuja/Dhammacakka	19 Jul	9 Jul	28 Jul	16 Jul	5 Jul
Losar – The Tibetan New Year	8 Feb	27 Feb	17 Feb	6 Feb	25 Jan
Rains Retreat	July – Oct every year				
Kathina	Oct – Nov every year (after Rains Retreat)				
Day of Enlightenment of the Buddha (Mahayana tradition)	15 Dec	15 Dec	15 Dec	15 Dec	15 Dec

Note: All variable dates are approximations only and would, therefore, need to be verified every year (see page 8).

Jain Festival – Dates

	1997	1998	1999	2000	2001
Paryushana	31 Aug	20 Aug	8 Sep	28 Aug	18 Aug

Baha'i Holy Days – Dates

Feast of Ridvan (Declaration of Baha'u'llah)	21 Apr–2 May
Declaration of the Bab	23 May
Ascension of Baha'u'llah	29 May
Martyrdom of the Bab	9 Jul
Birth of the Bab	20 Oct
Birth of Baha'u'llah	12 Nov
Day of the Covenant	26 Nov
Ascension of Abdu'l-Baha	28 Nov
Period of the Fast	19 days beginning 2 Mar
Feast of Naw-Ruz (Baha'i New Year)	21 Mar

Chinese Festivals – Dates

	1997	1998	1999	2000	2001
New Year	6 Feb	28 Jan	16 Feb	5 Feb	24 Jan
Qingming	5 Apr	5 Apr	5 Apr	4 Apr	5 Apr
Dragon Boat Festival	9 Jun	30 May	18 Jun	6 Jun	25 Jun
Mid-Autumn Festival	16 Sep	5 Oct	24 Sep	12 Sep	1 Oct
Chong Yang	10 Oct	28 Oct	17 Oct	6 Oct	25 Oct
Animal Signs	**Ox**	**Tiger**	**Hare**	**Dragon**	**Snake**

1997 to 2001
Calendars

KEY

B	=	Baha'i
Bd	=	Buddhist
C	=	Christian
Ch	=	Chinese
GB	=	Great Britain
H	=	Hindu
I	=	Israeli
Int	=	International
J	=	Japanese
Jai	=	Jain
Jw	=	Jewish
K	=	State of Kerala
M	=	Muslim
Sec	=	Secular
S	=	Sikh
SL	=	Sri Lanka
T	=	Tibetan
Th	=	Thai
US	=	USA

1997

	January	February	March
1	New Year's Day (C)/Ganjitsu (J)	St Brigid's Day (C)	St David's Day (C) ....
2	....	Candlemas Day (C)	Period of the Fast (for 19 days) (B)
3	....	Setsubon (J)	Hina Matsuri (J) ....
4	....	Lailat-ul-Qadr (M)	....
5	....	....	....
6	Epiphany (C)	Chinese New Year (Ox) (Ch)	....
7	Eastern Orthodox Christmas (C)	....	Mahasivaratri (H) ....
8	....	Losar (Bd/T)	....
9	....	Eid-ul-Fitr (M)	Mothering Sunday (C) ....
10	Ramadhan 1st (M)	....	....
11	....	Vasanta/Basant Panchami (S/H) ...... Shrove Tuesday (C)	....
12	Lohri (H/S)	Ash Wednesday (C)	....
13	Makara Sankrant/Pongal (H)	....	....
14	Eastern Orthodox New Year (C)	....	....
15	Birthday of Guru Gobind Singh (S)....	Mahaparinirvana (Bd)	....
16	....	....	....
17	....	....	St Patrick's Day (C) ....
18	....	....	....
19	Christian Unity Week begins (C)	....	....
20	....	....	....
21	....	Maghapuja (Bd)	Baha'i New Year (B) ....
22	Tu B'Shevat (Jw)	....	....
23	....	....	Palm Sunday (C)/Purim (Jw) ....
24	....	....	Holi (H/S) ....
25	....	....	....
26	....	....	....
27	....	....	....
28	....	....	Good Friday (C) ....
29	....		Holy Saturday (C) ....
30	....		Easter Sunday (C) ....
31	....		....

1997

	April	May	June
1	April Fool's Day (Sec)	May Day (Int)	
2			
3			
4			
5	Qingming (Ch)	Boys' Festival (J)	
6			
7			
8	Birthday of the Buddha (Bd) Mahayana tradition	Muharram (M) Ascension Day (C)	
9			Dragon Boat Festival (Ch) Martyrdom of Guru Arjan Dev (S)
10			
11			Shavuot 1st Day (Jw)
12		Christian Aid Week begins (C)	Shavuot 2nd Day (Jw)
13	Sinhala and Tamil New Year (SL) Songkrar Day (Thai New Year) (Th) Vaisakhi/Baisakhi (S/H)		
14	Vishu (H)		
15			
16	Ramnavami (H)		
17		Ashuraa (M)	
18	Eid-ul-Adha (M)	Pentecost Day /Whit Sunday (C)	
19			
20		Vesak (Theravada tradition) (Bd)	Poson (Bd)
21	Feast of Ridvan until 2 May (B)		
22	Passover/Pesach (1st Day) (Jw)		
23	St George's Day (C) Passover/Pesach (2nd Day) (Jw)	Declaration of the Bab (B)	
24			
25			
26			
27			
28	Passover/Pesach 7th Day (Jw)		
29	Passover/Pesach 8th Day (Jw)	Ascension of Baha'u'llah B) Corpus Christi (C)	Sts Peter and Paul (C)
30			
31			

1997

	July	August	September
1			
2			
3			
4			
5			
6			Ganesh Chathurthi (H)
7			
8			
9	Martyrdom of the Bab (B)		
10			
11			
12			
13			
14			
15		Assumption of the Blessed Virgin (C)	Onam (Sec)
16			Mid-Autumn Festival (Ch)
17	Milad-un-Nabi (M)		
18		Rakshabandhan (H)	
19	Asalhapuja/Dhammacakka (Bd)		
20			
21			
22			
23			
24		Janmashtami (H)	
25			
26			
27			
28			Harvest Festival (C)
29			
30			
31		Paryushana (Jai)	

1997

	October	November	December
1		All Saints' Day (C)	
2	Rosh Hashanah (1st Day) (Jw)	All Souls' Day (C)	
3	Rosh Hashanah (2nd Day) (Jw)		
4			Martytdom of Guru Teg Bahadur (S)
5		Guy Fawkes Day (GB)	
6			
7			
8			
9			
10	Chong Yang (Ch)		
11	Dassera (H)/Yom Kippur (Jw)		
12		Birth of Baha'u'llah (B)	
13			
14		Birthday of Guru Nanak (S)	Shab-e-Barat (M)
15			Day of Enlightenment of the Buddha (Mahayana tradition) (Bd)
16	Succot (1st Day) (Jw)		
17	Succot (2nd Day) (Jw)		
18			
19	Karva Chauth (H)		
20	Birth of the Bab (B)		
21			
22			
23	Succot (8th Day) (Jw)		
24	Simchat Torah (Jw)		Chanucah (1st Day) (Jw)
25			Christmas Day (C)
26		Shab-e-Miraj (M) Day of the Covenant (B)	St Stephen's Day (C) Boxing Day (GB)
27		Thanksgiving Day (US)	
28		Ascension of Abdu'l-Baha (B)	
29			
30	Deepawali/Diwali (H/S)	St Andrew's Day (C) First Sunday of Advent (C)	
31	Hallowe'en (Sec)		Ramadhan 1st (M)

1998

	January	February	March
1	New Year's Day (C) .... Ganjitsu (J)	Vasanta/Basant Panchami (H/S) ...... St Brigid's Day (C)	St David's Day (C) ....
2	....	Candlemas Day (C)	Period of the Fast (for 19 days) (B)
3	....	Setsubon (J)	Hina Matsuri (J) ....
4	....	....	....
5	....	....	....
6	Epiphany (C)	....	....
7	Eastern Orthodox Christmas (C)	....	....
8	....	....	....
9	....	....	....
10	....	....	....
11	....	Tu B'Shevat (I)/Maghapuja (Bd)	....
12	....	....	Purim (Jw) ....
13	Lohri (H/S)	....	....
14	Makara Sankrant/Pongal (H) .... Eastern Orthodox New Year (C)	....	Holi (H/S).......................................
15	....	Mahaparinirvana (Bd)	....
16	....	....	....
17	....	....	St Patrick's Day (C) ....
18	Christian Unity Week begins (C)	....	....
19	....	....	....
20	....	....	....
21	....	....	Baha'i New Year (B) ....
22	....	....	Mothering Sunday (C) ....
23	....	....	....
24	....	Shrove Tuesday (C)	....
25	Lailat-ul-Qadr (M)	Mahasivaratri (H).............................. Ash Wednesday (C)	....
26	....	....	....
27	....	Losar (Bd/T)	....
28	Chinese New Year (Tiger) (Ch)	....	....
29	....		....
30	Eid-ul-Fitr (M)		....
31	....		....

1998

April	May	June
1 April Fool's Day (Sec)	May Day (Int)	Shavuot 2nd Day (Jw)
2		
3		
4		
5 Ramnavami (H)/Qingming (Ch) Palm Sunday (C)	Boys' Festival (J)	
6		
7 Eid-ul-Adha (M)	Ashuraa (M)	Milad-un-Nabi (M)
8 Birthday of the Buddha (Bd) Mahayana tradition		
9		
10 Good Friday (C)	Christian Aid Week begins (C) Vesak (Theravada tradition) (Bd)	Poson (Bd)
11 Holy Saturday (C) Passover/Pesach (1st Day) (Jw)		Corpus Christi (C)
12 Easter Sunday (C) Passover/Pesach (2nd Day) (Jw)		
13 Vaisakhi/Baisakhi (S/H) Sinhala and Tamil New Year (SL) Songkrar Day (Thai New Year) (Th)		
14 Vishu (H)		
15		
16		
17 Passover/Pesach (7th Day) (Jw)		
18 Passover/Pesach (8th Day) (Jw)		
19		
20		
21 Feast of Ridvan until 2 May (B)	Ascension Day (C)	
22		
23 St George's Day (C)	Declaration of the Bab (B)	
24		
25		
26		
27		
28 Muharram (M)		
29	Martyrdom of Guru Arjan Dev (S) Ascension of Baha'u'llah B)	Sts Peter and Paul (C)
30	Dragon Boat Festival (Ch)	
31	Shavuot 1st Day (Jw) Pentecost Day/Whit Sunday (C)	

1998

	July	August	September
1			
2			
3			
4			
5			
6			
7			
8		Rakshabandhan (H)	
9	Martyrdom of the Bab (B) Asalhapuja/Dhammacakka (Bd)		
10			
11			
12			
13			
14		Janmashtami (H)	
15		Assumption of the Blessed Virgin (C)	
16			
17			
18			
19			
20		Paryushana (Jai)	
21			Rosh Hashanah 1st Day (Jw)
22			Rosh Hashanah 2nd Day (Jw)
23			
24			
25			
26		Ganesh Chaturthi (H)	
27			Harvest Festival (C)
28			
29			
30			Yom Kippur (Jw)
31			

1998

October	November	December
1	Dassera (H)	All Saints' Day (C)	....
2	....	All Souls' Day (C)	....
3	....	....	Shab-e-Barat (M) ....
4	....	Birthday of Guru Nanak (S)	....
5	Succot 1st Day (Jw) .... Mid-Autumn Festival (Ch)	Guy Fawkes Day (GB)	....
6	Succot 2nd Day (Jw)	....	....
7	....	....	....
8	Karva Chauth (H)	....	....
9	....	....	....
10	....	....	....
11	....	....	....
12	Succot 8th Day (Jw)	Birth of Baha'u'llah (B)	....
13	Simchat Torah (Jw)	....	....
14	....	....	Chanucah 1st Day (Jw) ....
15	....	....	Day of Enlightenment of the Buddha (Mahayana tradition) (Bd) .....
16	....	Shab-e-Miraj (M)	....
17	....	....	....
18	....	....	....
19	Deepawali/Diwali (H/S)	....	....
20	Birth of the Bab (B)	....	Ramadhan 1st (M) ....
21	....	....	....
22	....	....	....
23	....	....	....
24	....	Martyrdom of Guru Teg Bahadur (S)	....
25	....	....	Christmas Day (C) .... Birthday of Guru Gobind Singh (S)
26	....	Day of the Covenant (B) .... Thanksgiving Day (US)	St Stephen's Day (C) .... Boxing Day (GB)
27	....	....	....
28	Chong Yang (Ch)	Ascension of Abdu'l-Baha (B)	....
29	....	First Sunday of Advent (C)	....
30	....	St Andrew's Day (C)	....
31	Hallowe'en (Sec)		....

1999

	January	February	March
1	New Year's Day (C) .... Ganjitsu (J)	St Brigid's Day (C) .... Tu B'Shevat (I)	St David's Day (C) ....
2		Candlemas Day (C)	Period of the Fast (for 19 days) (B) Purim (Jw)/Maghapuja (Bd)
3		Setsubon (J)	Hina Matsuri (J)/Holi (H/S) ....
4			
5			
6	Epiphany (C)		
7	Eastern Orthodox Christmas (C)		
8			
9			
10			
11			
12			
13	Lohri (H/S)		
14	Makara Sankrant/Pongal (H) .... Lailat-ul-Qadr (M) Eastern Orthodox New Year (C)		Mothering Sunday (C) ....
15		Mahaparinirvana (Bd) .... Mahasivaratri (H)	
16		Shrove Tuesday (C) .... Chinese New Year (Hare) (Ch)	
17	Christian Unity Week begins (C)	Ash Wednesday (C) .... Losar (Bd/T)	St Patrick's Day (C) ....
18			
19	Eid-ul-Fitr (M)		
20			
21			Baha'i New Year (B) ....
22	Vasanta/Basant Panchami (S/H)		
23			
24			
25			Ramnavami (H) ....
26			
27			
28			Palm Sunday (C) .... Eid-ul-Adha (M)
29			
30			
31			

1999

	April	May	June
1	April Fool's Day (Sec) .... Passover/Pesach (1st Day) (Jw)	May Day (Int)	....
2	Good Friday (C) .... Passover/Pesach (2nd Day) (Jw)	....	....
3	Holy Saturday (C)	....	Corpus Christi (C) ....
4	Easter Sunday (C)	....	....
5	Qingming (Ch)	Boys' Festival (J)	....
6	....	....	....
7	Passover/Pesach (7th Day) (Jw)	....	....
8	Passover/Pesach (8th Day) (Jw) .... Birthday of the Buddha (Bd) Mahayana tradition	....	....
9	....	Christian Aid Week begins (C)	....
10	....	....	....
11	....	....	....
12	....	....	....
13	Sinhala and Tamil New Year (SL) .... Songkrar Day (Thai New Year) (Th)	Ascension Day (C)	....
14	Vaisakhi/Baisakhi (S/H) .... Vishu (H)	....	....
15	....	....	....
16	....	....	....
17	Muharram (M)	....	Martyrdom of Guru Arjan Dev (S) ...
18	....	....	Dragon Boat Festival (Ch) ....
19	....	....	....
20	....	....	....
21	Feast of Ridvan until 2 May (B)	Shavuot 1st Day (Jw)	....
22	....	Shavuot 2nd Day (Jw)	....
23	St George's Day (C)	Declaration of the Bab (B) .... Pentecost Day/Whit Sunday (C)	....
24	....	....	....
25	....	....	....
26	Ashuraa (M)	....	Milad-un-Nabi (M) ....
27	....	....	....
28	....	....	Poson (Bd) ....
29	....	Ascension of Baha'u'llah (B)	Sts Peter and Paul (C) ....
30	Vesak (Theravada tradition) (Bd)	....	
31		....	

1999

	July	August	September
1			
2			Janmashtami (H)
3			
4			
5			
6			
7			
8			Paryushana (Jai)
9	Martyrdom of the Bab (B)		
10			
11			Rosh Hashanah 1st Day (Jw)
12			Rosh Hashanah 2nd Day (Jw)
13			Ganesh Chaturthi (H)
14			
15		Assumption of the Blessed Virgin (C)	
16			
17			
18			
19			
20			Yom Kippur (Jw)
21			
22			
23			
24			Mid-Autumn Festival (Ch)
25			Succot 1st Day (Jw)
26		Rakshabandhan (H)	Harvest Festival (C) Succot 2nd Day (Jw)
27			
28	Asalhapuja/Dhammacakka (Bd)		
29			
30			
31			

1999

	October	November	December
1		All Saints' Day (C)	
2	Succot 8th Day (Jw)	All Souls' Day (C)	
3	Simchat Torah (Jw)		
4		Shab-e-Miraj (M)	Chanucah 1st Day (Jw)
5		Guy Fawkes Day (GB)	
6			
7		Deepawali/Diwali (H)	
8			
9			Ramadhan 1st (M)
10			
11			
12		Birth of Baha'u'llah (B)	
13			Martrydom of Guru Teg Bahadur (S)
14			
15			Day of Enlightenment of the Buddha (Mahayana tradition) (Bd)
16			
17	Chong Yang (Ch)		
18			
19	Dassera (H)		
20	Birth of the Bab (B)		
21			
22		Shab-e-Barat (M)	
23		Birthday of Guru Nanak (S)	
24			
25		Thanksgiving Day (US)	Christmas Day (C)
26		Day of the Covenant (B)	St Stephen's Day (C)
27	Karva Chauth (H)		Boxing Day (GB)
28		Ascension of Abdu'l-Baha (B) First Sunday of Advent (C)	
29			
30		St Andrew's Day (C)	
31	Hallowe'en (Sec)		

2000

January	February	March
1 New Year's Day (C) .... Ganjitsu (J)	St Brigid's Day (C)	St David's Day (C) ....
2	Candlemas Day (C)	Period of the Fast (for 19 days) (B)
3 Lailat-ul-Qadr (M)	Setsubon (J)	Hina Matsuri (J) ....
4	....	Mahasivaratri (H) ....
5	Chinese New Year (Dragon) (Ch)	....
6 Epiphany (C)	Losar (Bd/T)	....
7 Eastern Orthodox Christmas (C)	....	Shrove Tuesday (C) ....
8 Eid-ul-Fitr (M)	....	Ash Wednesday (C) ....
9	....	....
10	Vasanta/Basant Panchami (S/H)	....
11	....	....
12	....	....
13 Lohri (H/S)	....	....
14 Makara Sankrant/Pongal (H) .... Birthday of Guru Gobind Singh (S) Eastern Orthodox New Year (C)	....	....
15	Mahaparinirvana (Bd)	....
16 Christian Unity Week begins (C)	....	Eid-ul-Adha (M) ....
17	....	St Patrick's Day (C) ....
18	....	....
19	Maghapuja (Bd)	....
20	....	Purim (Jw) ....
21	....	Baha'i New Year (B) .... Holi (H/S)
22 Tu B'Shevat (I)	....	....
23	....	....
24	....	....
25	....	....
26	....	....
27	....	....
28	....	....
29	....	....
30		....
31		....

2000

	April	May	June
1	April Fool's Day (Sec)	May Day (Int)	Ascension Day (C) ....
2	....	....	....
3	....	....	....
4	Qingming (Ch)	....	....
5	....	Boys' Festival (J)	Martyrdom of Guru Arjan Dev (S) ...
6	Muharram (M)	....	Dragon Boat Festival (Ch) ....
7	....	....	....
8	Birthday of the Buddha (Bd) .... Mahayana tradition	....	....
9	Mothering Sunday (C)	....	Shavuot 1st Day (Jw) ....
10	....	....	Shavuot 2nd Day (Jw) ....
11	....	....	Pentecost Day/Whit Sunday (C) ....
12	Ramnavami (H)	....	....
13	Sinhala and Tamil New Year (SL) .... Songkrar Day (Thai New Year) (Th) Vaisakhi/Baisakhi (S/H)	....	....
14	Vishu (H)	Christian Aid Week begins (C)	....
15	Ashuraa (M)	....	Milad-un-Nabi (M) ....
16	Palm Sunday (C)	....	Poson (Bd) ....
17	....	....	....
18	....	Vesak (Theravada tradition) (Bd)	....
19	....	....	....
20	Passover/Pesach 1st Day (Jw)	....	....
21	Feast of Ridvan until 2 May (B) .... Passover/Pesach 2nd Day (Jw) Good Friday (C)	....	....
22	Holy Saturday (C)	....	Corpus Christi (C) ....
23	Easter Sunday (C) .... St George's Day (C)	Declaration of the Bab (B)	....
24	....	....	....
25	....	....	....
26	Passover/Pesach 7th Day (Jw)	....	....
27	Passover/Pesach 8th Day (Jw)	....	....
28	....	....	....
29	....	Ascension of Baha'u'llah (B)	Sts Peter and Paul (C) ....
30	....	....	....
31		....	

2000

	July	August	September
1			Ganesh Chaturthi (H)
2			
3			
4			
5			
6			
7			
8			
9	Martyrdom of the Bab (B)		
10			
11			
12			Mid-Autumn Festival (Ch)
13			
14			
15		Rakshabandhan (H) Assumption of the Blessed Virgin (C)	
16	Asalhapuja/Dhammacakka (Bd)		
17			
18			
19			
20			
21			
22		Janmashtami (H)	
23			
24			Harvest Festival (C)
25			
26			
27			
28		Paryushana (Jai)	
29			
30			Rosh Hashana 1st Day (Jw)
31			

2000

	October	November	December
1	Rosh Hashanah 2nd Day (Jw)	All Saints' Day (C)	Martyrdom of Guru Teg Bahadur (S)
2	....	All Souls' Day (C)	....
3	....	....	First Sunday of Advent (C) ....
4	....	....	....
5	....	Guy Fawkes Day (GB)	....
6	Chong Yang (Ch)	....	....
7	Dassera (H)	....	....
8	....	....	....
9	Yom Kippur (Jw)	....	....
10	....	Shab-e-Barat (M)	....
11	....	Birthday of Guru Nanak (S)	....
12	....	Birth of Baha'u'llah (B)	....
13	....	....	....
14	Succot 1st Day (Jw)	....	....
15	Succot 2nd Day (Jw)	....	Day of Enlightenment of the Buddha (Mahayana tradition) (Bd) .....
16	Karva Chauth (H)	....	....
17	....	....	....
18	....	....	....
19	....	....	....
20	Birth of the Bab (B)	....	....
21	Succot 8th Day (Jw)	....	....
22	Simchat Torah (Jw)	....	Chanucah 1st Day (Jw) ....
23	....	Thanksgiving Day (US)	....
24	Shab-e-Miraj (M)	....	....
25	....	....	Christmas Day (C) ....
26	Deepawali/Diwali (H/S)	Day of the Covenant (B)	St Stephen's Day (C) .... Boxing Day (GB)
27	....	Ramadhan 1st (M)	....
28	....	Ascension of Abdu'l-Baha (B)	....
29	....	....	....
30	....	St Andrew's Day (C)	....
31	Hallowe'en (Sec)		....

2001

	January	February	March
1	New Year's Day (C) .... Ganjitsu (J)	St Brigid's Day (C)	St David's Day (C) ....
2	....	Candlemas Day (C)	Period of the Fast (for 19 days) (B)
3	....	Setsubon (J)	Hina Matsuri (J) ....
4	....	....	....
5	....	....	....
6	Epiphany (C)	....	....
7	Eastern Orthodox Christmas (C)	....	....
8	....	Tu B'Shevat (I) .... Maghapuja (Bd)	....
9	....	....	Purim (Jw) ....
10	....	....	Holi (H/S) ....
11	....	....	....
12	....	....	....
13	Lohri (H/S) .... Makara Sankrant/Pongal (H)	....	....
14	Eastern Orthodox New Year (C)	....	....
15	....	Mahaparinirvana (Bd)	....
16	....	....	....
17	....	....	St Patrick's Day (C) ....
18	....	....	....
19	....	....	....
20	....	....	....
21	Christian Unity Week begins (C)	Mahasivaratri (H)	Baha'i New Year (B) ....
22	....	....	....
23	....	....	....
24	Chinese New Year (Snake) (Ch)	....	....
25	Losar (Bd/T)	....	Mothering Sunday (C) ....
26	....	....	....
27	....	Shrove Tuesday (C)	....
28	....	Ash Wednesday (C)	....
29	Vasanta/Basant Panchami (S/H)		....
30	....		....
31	....		....

2001

	April	May	June
1	April Fool's Day (Sec)	May Day (Int)	....
2	Ramnavami (H)	....	....
3	....	....	Pentecost Day/Whit Sunday (C) ....
4	....	....	....
5	Qingming (Ch)	Boys' Festival (J)	....
6	....	....	Poson (Bd) ....
7	....	Vesak (Theravada tradition) (Bd)	....
8	Palm Sunday (C) .... Passover/Pesach 1st Day (Jw) Birthday of the Buddha (Bd) Mahayana tradition	....	....
9	Passover/Pesach 2nd Day (Jw)	....	....
10	....	....	....
11	....	....	....
12	....	....	....
13	Vaisakhi/Baisakhi (S/H) Sinhala and Tamil New Year (SL) Good Friday (C) Songkrar Day (Thai New Year) (Th)	Christian Aid Week begins (C)	....
14	Vish u (H) .... Holy Saturday (C) Passover/Pesach 7th Day (Jw)	....	Corpus Christi (C) ....
15	Easter Sunday (C) .... Passover/Pesach 8th Day (Jw)	....	....
16	....	....	....
17	....	....	....
18	....	....	....
19	....	....	....
20	....	....	....
21	Feast of Ridvan until 2 May (B)	....	....
22	....	....	....
23	St George's Day (C)	Declaration of the Bab (B)	....
24	....	Ascension Day (C)	....
25	....	....	Dragon Boat Festival (Ch) ....
26	....	....	....
27	....	....	....
28	....	Shavuot 1st Day (Jw)	....
29	....	Ascension of Baha'u'llah (B) .... Shavuot 2nd Day (Jw)	Sts Peter and Paul (C) ....
30	....	....	....
31		....	

2001

	July	August	September
1			
2			
3			
4		Rakshabandhan (H)	
5	Asalhapuja/Dhammacakka (Bd)		
6			
7			
8			
9	Martyrdom of the Bab (B)		
10			
11			
12		Janmashtami (H)	
13			
14			
15		Assumption of The Blessed Virgin (C)	
16			
17			
18		Paryushana (Jai)	Rosh Hashanah 1st Day (Jw)
19			Rosh Hashanah 2nd Day (Jw)
20			
21			
22		Ganesh Chaturthi (H)	
23			
24			
25			
26			
27			Yom Kippur (Jw)
28			
29			
30			Harvest Festival (C)
31			

2001

	October	November	December
1	Mid-Autumn Festival (Ch)	All Saints' Day (C)	
2	Succot 1st Day (Jw)	All Souls' Day (C)	
3	Succot 2nd Day (Jw)		
4		Karva Chauth (H)	
5		Guy Fawkes Day (GB)	
6			
7			
8			
9	Succot 8th Day (Jw)		
10	Simchat Torah (Jw)		
11			
12		Birth of Baha'u'llah (B)	
13			
14		Deepawali/Diwali (H/S)	
15			Day of Enlightenment of the Buddha (Mahayana tradition) (Bd)
16			
17			
18			
19			
20	Birth of the Bab (B)		
21			
22		Thanksgiving Day (US)	
23			
24			
25	Chong Yang (Ch)		Christmas Day (C)
26	Dassera (H)	Day of the Covenant (B)	St Stephen's Day (C) Boxing Day (GB)
27			
28		Ascension of Abdu'l-Baha (B)	
29			
30		St Andrew's Day (C) Chanucah 1st Day (Jw) Birthday of Guru Nanak (S)	
31	Hallowe'en (Sec)		

Index of Festivals

KEY

B	=	Baha'i
Bd	=	Buddhist
C	=	Christian
Ch	=	Chinese
GB	=	Great Britain
H	=	Hindu
I	=	Israeli
Int	=	International
J	=	Japanese
Jai	=	Jain
Jw	=	Jewish
K	=	State of Kerala
M	=	Muslim
Sec	=	Secular
S	=	Sikh
SL	=	Sri Lanka
T	=	Tibetan
Th	=	Thai
US	=	USA

General Index